SUGAR
for
THE HOUSE

SUGAR
— *for* —
THE HOUSE

A HISTORY OF EARLY SUGAR REFINING
IN NORTH WEST ENGLAND

MONA DUGGAN

FONTHILL

Fonthill Media Limited
Fonthill Media LLC
www.fonthillmedia.com
office@fonthillmedia.com

First published in 2013

British Library Cataloguing in Publication Data:
A catalogue record for this book is available from the British Library

ISBN 978-1-78155-040-3

Typeset in 10.5pt on 15pt Sabon LT
Printed and bound in England

Connect with us
 facebook.com/fonthillmedia twitter.com/fonthillmedia

Contents

Abbreviations:

ND	No date is cited
THSLC	Transactions of the Historic Society of Lancashire and Cheshire
RSLC	The Record Society of Lancashire and Cheshire
CNWRS	Centre for North West Regional Studies
CS	Chetham Society
CRO	Chester Record Office
LRO	Lancashire Record Office (Lancashire Archives)

Preface

My interest in sugar refining was fired by the discovery of an early sugar refinery operating in a cottage in the market town of Ormskirk in the 1680s. It was a very small concern employing only one refiner who understood the 'art and mystery of sugar refining', and who was financed by the local innkeeper and his family. I wondered whether this one small enterprise had played a part in the foundations of the giant sugar refining firms that dominated Liverpool's dockland during the early twentieth century. A reference in the book *Sugar* assured me that, 'Sugar used to be refined … in scores of little refineries all over Britain'.[1] If this was the case, I decided to trace the growth of these small refineries before the arrival of the major firms that controlled the sugar industry in the North West during the nineteenth and twentieth centuries.

I was surprised how quickly refineries for West Indian sugar were established. The cane plant had been introduced to the British colonies in the West Indies only fifty years before the establishment of the Ormskirk refinery, and yet the basic refining process had taken several years to perfect. Problems also had to be solved involving the transportation the raw sugar across the Atlantic, and finding suitable places to dock and to unload the barrels. It seemed incredible that within fifty years, the demand for West Indian sugar had increased so much that it was thought worthwhile to set up a refinery in Ormskirk, a town that was a most unsuitable place for the industry both geographically and historically.

If it was considered feasible to establish a sugar refinery in Ormskirk, what was happening elsewhere in the North West? Had the industry been established successfully in other towns? What type of people had chosen to invest in an industry that was completely new to the area? Why had they established the industry in certain North West towns and not in others? Was their confidence rewarded in the seventeenth and eighteenth centuries, before the new, gigantic firms emerged and dominated the northern sugar industry?

These questions prompted me to explore the trade in sugar. When did it originate? Which people first realised the potential value of the sweet tasting sap of the sugar cane, primarily as a medicine and later as a food, and who experimented with the refining process? Which other countries had taken part in the development of the product throughout the centuries? The cane sugar industry was established in the West Indies when the New World was colonised, but where were the first refineries? Where did the small refinery in Ormskirk fit into the global development of the sugar industry?

It was to address these problems that I embarked on this study. As I researched the establishment of local refineries, I found it was virtually impossible to find a consecutive account of sugar refining in any of the North West towns, so I adopted a 'jackdaw' approach to the problem, picking up snippets of information wherever I could find them, and piecing them together to trace the birth and early development of the sugar refining industry in the North West. By this method, I discovered the location of many of the earliest refineries in the area, and the identity of the pioneers who had the confidence to invest in this industry that was completely new to the region in the seventeenth century.

As the study proceeded, I found that the small refineries established in the North West had a very important role in the emergence of the British sugar industry. Their progress provided a fascinating glimpse into the introduction to the region of a new industry, which was to become one of the cornerstones of Lancashire's success as an industrial centre. Perhaps what was even more important was the fact that this industry was to attract ever-increasing investment into the infrastructure of the region.

Frequently, it is claimed that the economic boom that the North West experienced in the eighteenth and nineteenth centuries was the result of the slave trade. However, I would argue instead that it was the result of the expansion of the sugar industry. Of course, slaves were a feature in the later development of the industry, but it was to supply the needs of the sugar industry that the first docks were constructed in Liverpool, the Mersey was made navigable to serve Warrington, and the Irwell was cleared to serve Manchester. The roads of the region were also upgraded to enable sugar and coal to be transported to the refineries, and also to facilitate the delivery of refined sugar to customers in the inland towns. It was these improvements in the infrastructure of the area that enabled other industries to prosper, and it was primarily to meet the demands of the sugar industry that they were undertaken. The slave trade, which developed when there was a shortage of white indentured servants in the West Indies, was yet another outcome of the boom in the sugar industry, which in my opinion, was responsible for much of the economic success of the North West in the nineteenth century.

In fact the sugar industry, together with others such as the tobacco and cotton industries whose basic raw materials also came from overseas, made a major contribution to the economic boom experienced by the whole of the British Isles in the late eighteenth and nineteenth centuries. As L. A. G. Strong commented, by the end of the eighteenth century the sugar industry 'was no longer merely a matter of interest to private individuals. It had become a source of public wealth and was therefore of national importance'.[2] Refined sugar was exported in great quantities to Europe and to the emerging colonies, and was one of those industries that 'formed the basis of re-exports of enormous value'.[3] It was these exports that prompted the development of similar industries in Australia and South Africa, where colonists were determined to have a part in this lucrative trade.

Thus, these small ventures into a new industry in the North West were to prosper, expand, and combine to become the basis of a world-wide industry of immense proportions. It is these ventures, as they expand, contract, and finally concentrate in Liverpool, making it the centre of sugar refining in the North West, that are to be studied and traced in the following chapters.

CHAPTER 1

Introducing the Sugar Industry

Growing the Cane

The sweetening properties of the sugar cane have been known since classical times, when the plant was recorded in the writings of Herodotus, Theophrastus, and Seneca. The Indians extracted the juice from the plant as early as 500 BC, and the cane was grown in China 200 years before the coming of Christ. We know little about the way these people processed the cane, nor indeed what use they made of the juice. However in early Christian times, sugar was used as a medicine by the people of the Middle East, who regarded it as a remedy for the plague, jaundice, and for chest complaints. From the sixth century, the cane was grown both in Persia and around the Mediterranean basin by the Arabs and Egyptians, who exported sugar to other regions.[4] In fact, remains of the pots used by the Persians for the refining process were discovered by French archaeologists during excavations in Iran. By the Middle Ages, sugar loaves from India and Arabia were being exported to England and sold mainly for medicinal uses.[5] However, according to a Parisian author of a cookery book in 1392, sugar was sprinkled very sparingly on food to improve the flavour, in a similar way to the use made of expensive spices.[6]

During medieval times, sugar cane was cultivated by peasants on their small holdings, and also by tenants who leased parts of large estates surrounding the Mediterranean, and who surrendered some of their crop to the landowners in return both for the use of the land and of the equipment they needed. This method of farming ceased after the Crusades, when most of the Mediterranean lands passed into the hands of Western feudal lords. They imposed their traditional farming methods on the cultivation of sugar cane. It was planted on the demesne lands, and the peasants provided the labour as part of their feudal dues. This reorganisation was necessary because of the large capital investment that was needed to grow and process the crop, and so meet the ever-increasing demands of the commercial market.[7]

During the fourteenth century, much of the sugar supplied to England was grown in Egypt and was exported from the port of Alexandria, whence it was shipped to Venice. There, it was re-exported to England, and sold at prices varying from 1s per lb in the twelfth century to 1s 7d per lb in the thirteenth. At this time, its use was still mainly medicinal. For instance in 1353, King John I of France ordered the apothecaries of Paris not to substitute honey for sugar in their 'confections'. In fact, the use of sugar as a medicine continued until Stuart times in Lancashire. For example in 1614, after the death of Robert Jump of North Meols near Southport, it was recorded in the probate documents that his administrator Anne Jump had 'paid and contented for wine and shuger spent by the decedent [in] his sickness time 2s 2d'.[8]

As the trade expanded, new ways of processing the cane were invented. One important invention was the three-roller vertical mill that crushed the cane, and was constructed in 1449 by a Sicilian farmer. This method was used to extract the juice from the cane until the seventeenth century, long after the cane fields of Egypt had been abandoned and the cultivation of sugar had moved away from the Mediterranean lands to the Caribbean islands.

As Spain and Portugal expanded overseas, they introduced sugar cane into the lands that they had conquered. In fact, Columbus is credited with introducing the crop into the West Indies on his second voyage across the Atlantic in 1493. It had already been planted in Madeira in 1420, followed by plantings in Domingo in 1494, the Canary Islands in 1503, Mexico in 1520, and then in various West Indian Islands in the sixteenth century.[9] The Portuguese also grew the crop successfully on the north coast of Brazil around the towns of Bahia and Pernambuco, and by 1600, the Portuguese had become the chief suppliers to the European market.

A three-roller vertical mill and sugar boiling plant. A pipe took the extracted juice across to the boilers. (*Dunn*, Sugar and Slaves, *p. 193*)

   This made their ships the prime targets for Elizabethan privateers. Sugar was such a valuable commodity that it was regarded as very desirable booty, and as sugar was carried in a partially refined state in large barrels or hogsheads, it was easy for pirates to transfer their booty from one ship to another. It was said that this illegal 'trade' was so successful that sugar was cheaper in London than in Lisbon or even in the West Indies.[10]

   Sugar cane is perishable and bulky, and so the initial refining processes were done near the cane fields. In the past, there was always the danger that the sugar might be damaged by sea water while it was in transit across the Atlantic. Consequently, importers preferred to complete the refining process nearer to their final markets in Europe. It was also difficult for them to obtain sufficient fuel and clean water for the process near the cane fields. Therefore, refineries were set up in several European

Gathering sugar cane in Madeira. (*Alberto Viera & Francisco Clode,* The Sugar Route in Madeira, *p. 40*)

ports, Venice being one of the earliest. Antwerp, Amsterdam, and London followed later as the West Indian trade became established. During the reign of Henry VIII, Venetian traders brought sugar to England, and the earliest refineries were set up in London. The London historian John Stowe (1525-1605) reported that:

> There were but two sugar houses. And their profit was but little, by reason there were so many sugar bakers in Antwerp. And sugar came thence better and cheaper than it could be afforded in London. And for the space of twenty years together these two sugar houses served the whole realm, both to the commendation and profit of them that undertook the same, whose benefit was occasioned by the stoppage of intercourse between England and Antwerp.[11]

Remains of sugar moulds dating from the sixteenth century have been found in the valley of the River Fleet in London and in Southwark. Possibly, these were the sites of the two early English refineries, or if not, the sites of the potteries where the moulds were made for those refineries. Unfortunately, the report of the discovery did not reveal whether they were made of local clay or whether the moulds had been imported. Certainly, some seventeenth century examples that were found in Southampton and Plymouth originated in either Spain or Portugal, for they were made from dark red clay that came from those areas.

In the early seventeenth century, the supremacy of the Portuguese in the sugar trade was challenged by the Dutch, who were very successful in establishing the crop in Surinam on the north-west coast of South America. In 1630, the Dutch seized control of Pernambuco from the Portuguese, and it was at that time that refineries were opened in Amsterdam. Meanwhile, the English sought ways to establish a foothold in the valuable trade. Sir Walter Raleigh (1552-1618) investigated the possibility of establishing settlements in the Guianas in 1595, but that proved impossible. The merchant and adventurer Captain Charles Leigh (d. 1605) tried to set up a settlement on the River Waiapoco, but that attempt did not succeed. Sugar cane was planted on the West Indian island of Bermuda in 1616, but the climatic conditions did not suit the crop.[12] It was not until 1627, when the first settlers in Barbados planted sugar cane that they had bought from the Dutch at Surinam, that some success was achieved cultivating sugar in the British West Indian. However, the planters still had no idea how to process the cane, and so they accepted an offer from the Indians who lived in the Dutch colony to teach them how to make a sweet refreshing drink from their new crop. Of course, the settlers had more ambitious plans, and finally managed to persuade the Dutch settlers to teach them how to process the juice. Then the crude sugar was sold to the Dutch merchants, who took it back to Amsterdam for further refining. This link with Amsterdam proved very advantageous for the English planters during the 1640s when the Civil War disrupted all trade in England. Throughout the war, the sugar planters were able to continue to sell their sugar to the merchants in Amsterdam to be processed, and also to sell it in mainland Europe.

When the Civil War was over, various Navigation Acts dating from 1651 were passed. By these laws, Parliament exerted control over the

English sugar trade and successfully destroyed the Dutch monopoly. The colonies were to use only English ships, and were to trade exclusively with English merchants through English ports. Prohibitive tariffs were imposed on foreign sugar entering England, and although sugar from the colonies was also taxed when it entered England, it was at a much lower rate. Taxes were also imposed to discourage refining in the colonies; for instance, in 1651 colonial muscovado – unrefined sugar – was taxed at 1s 6d per cwt, while the rate for semi-refined sugar was 5s per cwt. Another similar concession to benefit the refiners was the rebate of tax when the sugar had been refined and was then re-exported to the continent. These protectionist measures were very successful and the English sugar refining industry prospered. In fact, trade with western Europe increased so dramatically that by 1700, the English planters were supplying almost half of all the sugar consumed in that area.

The expansion of cane fields at first into Madeira and the Canary Islands, and then by the seventeenth century into the Caribbean islands, brought the price of legitimate sugar – not the product of piracy – tumbling down. In fact by the 1680s, it was selling in England at about 4d per lb. The English had always been partial to sugar, and in Tudor times it was regarded as a great delicacy. For instance, the Liverpool Town Book of 1576 recorded that during the celebrations for the nineteenth anniversary of the accession of Queen Elizabeth, 'Mayster maior departed to his owne house, accompanied of the saide alderman and others, a great numbre, upon whom he did bestow sack and other whyte wyne and sugar liberally.'[13] As the falling price brought sugar within reach of the whole population, the diet of the ordinary people changed, and the consumption of fruit that was sweetened with sugar increased significantly.[14]

As the demand for sugar soared, the planters in Barbados, whose original crop had been tobacco, realised that more profit could be made from producing cane. Consequently, they increased the size of their fields by combining various holdings, and as the need for more labour arose, they expanded their workforce by acquiring more indentured servants. Most of these workers in the seventeenth century came from Europe; in fact many were from North West England. For instance in 1648, Liverpool Borough Council decided to round up poor children and beggars from the streets and send them to Barbados as indentured servants.[15] Similarly in 1699, the overseers of the poor in Aughton, near Ormskirk, arranged for two orphans John Woods and Joshua Taylor to be bound for seven and ten years respectively to Captain Clayton at St Kitts.[16] This was the usual procedure: the servants-to-be were indentured to the ship's captain, who then sold the indentures – and the servants – to the planters when he reached the West Indies.

Working conditions were very difficult in Barbados, and many servants suffered extremely harsh treatment. Consequently, once their indentures had expired – usually after seven years – many of the servants left the colony completely, while a few established independent plantations and refineries. This left the planters without a viable work force, because few people were willing to be bound as indentured servants once reports of conditions in the cane fields reached England. The problem was so severe that in 1696, an Act was passed in Barbados by the island's assembly offering £18 to anyone who imported either an English or Scottish man-servant to the island. A similar Act was passed in the Leeward Islands, offering 2,000 lb of sugar, worth about £10, for every man-servant brought to those islands 'and empowering the Governor to dispose of such servants among the planters to serve according to the terms of the … Act'. One solution suggested by the agents from the islands to the Council of Trade and Plantations in London, was that if the regiment and two companies stationed in St Christopher were disbanded, many of the men would stay there and apply themselves to planting.[17] Yet despite all these inducements, sufficient labourers could not be found to work on the plantations.

However, slaves from Africa had been employed by the Portuguese and later by the Dutch in their plantations, and consequently, when this acute need for labourers arose in the English colonies, the English planters decided to follow the example of their neighbours and bought slaves, at first from those other planters and later directly from the slave traders. This established the notorious English triangular trade of taking mixed cargoes to Africa, selling the goods to the natives, buying slaves, taking them to the West Indies, and selling them to the planters before returning to England with cargoes of sugar and rum. In fact by 1713, the Royal African Company had built eight forts on the African coast, and had transported 120,000 slaves to the Americas, and had imported 30,000 tons of sugar from the West Indies.[18]

In a cane field near Durban, Natal, South Africa.

Much later in the nineteenth century, the cultivation of sugar was introduced to both Australia and South Africa. In Australia during the 1860s, farmers began to include it among their other crops on Oxley Creek in the areas now known as Corinda and Chelmer near Brisbane. There were no sugar mills, and because transporting the bulky cane to the coast was a problem, 'a small sugar mill [was] placed on a punt, [and] went from place to place to crush the cane one stick at a time'.[19] Later, several farmers built a primitive mill similar to the one invented in Sicily in 1449. It had iron rollers 18 inches in diameter and 30 inches in length, placed vertically, and was operated using gears powered by a single horse. There were no roads to these remote farms, so the farmers used boats to take their produce for sale in Ipswich, where the merchants met them at the wharf. Their labours were rewarded when the large grained bright yellow sugar was sold at prices as high as £36 to £40 per ton. However, after 'a succession of severe winters that ruined their crops, the cane farmers decided to migrate northwards to the jungle covered, tropical coastal lands'.[20]

In South Africa, one of the earliest sugar growers was William Campbell of Muckleneuk in Natal. When he wrote home in 1861, he included an estimate of what it had cost him to establish his 70 acre plantation. He reckoned that he had spent £3,000 during his first year, and to do that, he had been forced to borrow £2,000. However, he was full of confidence and declared, 'We hope to pay off something like half this season and half the next, meantime we are really straitened, we have no money ... I am free to confess that our independence has caused us to be frequently sorely embarrassed.' Nevertheless, that was the price Campbell paid for being one of the pioneers who established the South African sugar industry, which still thrives today in Natal.[21]

Early Sugar Refining

At first, the sugar refining in Barbados was very crude. In fact Richard Ligon, who visited the colony in 1647, reported that the sugar was no more than bare muscovado, or unrefined sugar full of molasses, the kind of sugar that was taxed at the lower rate in 1651. Gradually, the English planters persuaded experienced refiners from both Brazil and Surinam to pass on their knowledge of refining. They spent three years experimenting with different processes, and at the end of that time, Ligon was able to report that the English were able to produce a very sweet, almost white sugar.

The first part of the process was very simple. The canes were fed through the three-roller vertical mills, turned either by water, wind, or horse power. They were passed first one way and then back again until as much juice as possible had been extracted from them. This was collected below the rollers and funnelled along troughs to copper or iron vats where it was boiled. Meanwhile, the trash or waste cane was carefully stacked ready for fuelling the next process.

It was at this stage that the skill of the sugar boiler was needed. Bullock's blood or lime water was added to the boiling mass, causing most of the impurities to rise and form a scum. This was ladled off and retained to be processed later into a very inferior sugar, which

Cattle providing the power to turn the sugar mill and crush the cane in Madeira. (*Viera & Clode*, The Sugar Route in Madeira, *p. 69*)

The crushing plant in Colombia in the late twentieth century. (*Photograph courtesy of Dr Audrey Coney*)

was almost black in colour. The clear juice was drawn off below the surface through a woollen straining cloth and run into a second vat, where the same process was repeated. Again, the clear juice was drawn off and the process was repeated about four times. Throughout these boilings, the sugar boiler had to monitor the temperature of the trash fires burning below the vats, because if they burnt too fiercely, the sugar would caramelise on the sides of the vats and the sugar would turn brown. Finally, using his judgement to choose the correct moment, the boiler allowed the sugar to crystallise by evaporating all the water. The crystalline sugar was then transferred to wooden trays or boxes, where it was stirred with a paddle until it cooled.

The sugar still contained a quantity of molasses, and during the early days of refining, this was separated from the sugar crystals by two different methods. The simplest way was to pack the sugar into a hogshead, a large barrel, which had holes in the bottom. The molasses gradually drained through these holes leaving a brownish sugar. The holes were then plugged and the hogsheads were ready for export. This product was known as muscovado, a cheap sugar often sold in the grocers' shops in England at that time.

The other method, which produced a whiter sugar, had been used in the Mediterranean lands since the twelfth century. By this method, once the sugar had been boiled, clarified, and crystallised, it was packed into conical porous clay pots. The sugar crystals were packed into the upper container and covered with damp clay. Syrup dripped into the lower container leaving pure white sugar loaf in the upper mould. Most of these moulds conformed to the same pattern, a conical shaped mould with a hole at the bottom to allow the molasses to drain out, and a jar to collect the syrup as it dripped through the hole. The only slight variations were the early Iranian and Egyptian moulds, which were shallower and often had three holes at the base of the mould. Some of the early jars had feet at the base, but this design was found to be impractical because the feet broke off in use. The interiors of the cones were smoothed in various ways to enable the dried sugar crystals to be collected easily from the cone. In later years, the interiors were covered with slip (a smooth, creamy clay), and in the nineteenth century, the moulds were made of glazed stoneware. The drip jars that collected the molasses had high shoulders, heavy rims, and sturdy, ring-footed bases.

Boiling sugar in the West Indies. (*Denis Diderot's* Encyclopedia, *written between 1750 and 1772*)

Boiling sugar in Colombia in the late-twentieth century. (*Photograph courtesy of Dr Audrey Coney*)

Cooling the boiled sugar in Colombia. (*Photograph courtesy of Dr Audrey Coney*)

Sugar moulds.

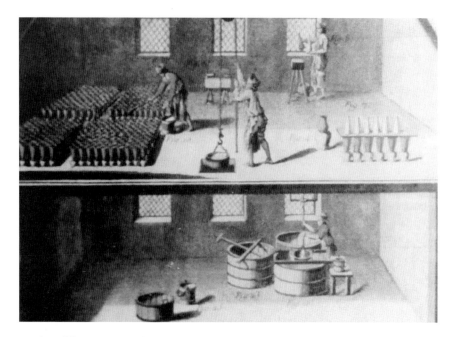

Workers filling sugar moulds and stacking them on the upper floor of a refinery. (*Denis Diderot's* Encyclopedia)

In the 1750s, a Swede, Angerstein, toured Britain, visiting as many industrial sites as he could. Some people regarded him as the equivalent of today's industrial spy and refused to admit him to their premises. However, he was allowed into a pottery where sugar moulds were made in Prescot, and he wrote a detailed account of the processes involved. The furnace was built in the same way as the usual pottery kilns, the only difference being that no 'chapsels' or clay supports were used for these larger vessels. The potters used brownish red clay that had been well kneaded, but had not been sieved through a cloth as it was for other pots. The moulds were thrown on a wheel, and Angerstein noted that 'a boy is also employed to furnish the motive power by winding a crank'. He continued to record both the sizes and the prices charged, facts that would have been of great interest to any competitors in Sweden or elsewhere. A mould, 2 feet 3 inches high with the capacity of ten gallons, would sell for 7*d*, while a smaller one, 1 feet 6 inches tall, and 9 inches in diameter, sold for 3*d*, and an even smaller one, standing 1 feet 3 inches, was sold for 2*s* 5*d*.[22] These moulds were produced as near as possible to the sites of the refineries to avoid the difficulties involved in transporting breakable pots.

The moulds were sealed at the top with wet clay, and as the water permeated through the sugar, it took with it most of the remaining impurities, leaving behind a much whiter sugar, particularly at the top of the mould. This process was repeated, often using smaller moulds, until a pure white sugar was obtained. The sugar produced in this way was known as clayed sugar, which could command a much higher price because of its purity and colour. However when it was imported, it also attracted a higher rate of tax in order to protect the trade of the refiners in Britain. As a consequence, most of the refiners in the West Indies ceased producing fine white sugar, and concentrated on increasing the quantity of muscovado for export.

Later in the eighteenth century, clayed sugar was thought to be the best kind of sugar for preserving fruit, and consequently, the price rose higher during the English fruit season. One of the advantages of refining sugar in Britain was that most of the molasses drained from the sugar could be used in the process of distilling rum and thus another profitable industry was provided with raw materials.[23]

Sugar moulds in a factory. (*Denis Diderot's* Encyclopedia)

The Sugar Trade in the North West

In the sixteenth and early seventeenth centuries, sugar was sold in the London market, refined, and then re-exported to the continent or distributed throughout England. In fact as late as 10 November 1725, Nicholas Blundell of Little Crosby, near Liverpool, recorded that 'a box came from London ... with tea, sugar etc. for use of the house'. Blundell still ordered sugar by bulk from London as his predecessors had done, despite the fact that by that time, Liverpool ships were trading directly with the West Indies and refineries had been established in the town.

Before railways and canals provided improved transport for bulky goods, most heavy goods were brought by sea to the North West, especially those from London. It is recorded that a vessel arrived in Liverpool from London in 1569 with a cargo of iron, tin, sugar, and other products, together valued at £1,000.[24] In fact, sugar was often included in the cargo of ships returning to the North West after carrying Cheshire cheese to London.[25] Despite this trade, fewer than twenty ships were actually based in Liverpool – a small port in the sixteenth century consisting of 7 streets with fewer than 300 houses. Those ships traded mainly with Ireland and the ports along the western coast of Britain.[26] However in the 1640s, that trade was reduced severely by the Irish rebellion of 1641, the Civil War, and finally by Cromwell's campaign in Ireland in 1649.

After the Restoration, some Liverpool merchants thought that the newly-found stability would mean an increase in trade with Ireland, and so they commissioned a dozen new ships to be built in readiness.[27] However, the Cavalier Parliament (1661-1678) had other ideas. They extended the Navigation Laws to prevent Irish livestock and dairy products being imported into England, and consequently, Ireland was forced to trade with other European countries. This resulted in a 10 per cent reduction of the English trade with Ireland, leaving the Liverpool merchants with new ships surplus to their requirements.

Then, when the plague struck London, that port was closed, and even more Liverpool ships were left idle, unable to trade with the capital. The Liverpool Port Books reveal that in July 1665, a London-based ship, the *Hunter*, brought sugar from the English plantations in Barbados into Liverpool. The owners of that cargo were Israel Fletcher, Jonathan Smith, and Richard Bradshaw, London merchants, who had been forced to divert their cargo to the North to avoid plague-stricken London. Perhaps it was the arrival of this cargo that alerted more of the Liverpool merchants to the opportunities of trading directly with the West Indies, or perhaps the London merchants decided to base their trade in Liverpool. Certainly George Fry, the master of the ship, established ties with Liverpool, for he married Margaret Tarleton, the daughter of one of the leading Liverpool merchants,[28] whose family later became sugar bakers with a refinery in the Castle Street area of Liverpool.[29]

Whatever the reason, the Liverpool merchants decided to use their newly redundant ships to trade directly with America and the West Indies for both tobacco and sugar. Probably one of the earliest voyages direct from Barbados to Liverpool was that of the *Antelope,* which docked in May 1665 carrying muscovado sugar from the English plantations for wealthy investors, including William Blundell, the 'Cavalier' of Little Crosby, William Grange and partners, and Edward Cranage. This cargo must have proved very profitable, for shortly afterwards, Blundell arranged for the *Antelope* to make another trip to Barbados. He was joined by several other gentlemen who also invested in the project.

Blundell recorded that Dr Sylvester Richmond had agreed to act as the agent for the voyage, and that among this group of investors was his cousin Henry Blundell of Ince Blundell. The two Blundells invested £40, and that entitled them to put their own cargo into a quarter of the cargo space of the little ship. William's sister Winifred wanted to join in the speculation, so William agreed that she could invest £5, one eighth of his own investment, and in return receive or lose one eighth of their profit or loss. The first problem was what to send to Barbados that could be sold at a good profit. William decided that linen cloth would sell well in the hot climate, and so he bought 3,332 yards, probably from Ormskirk market or directly from the weavers near his home in south-west Lancashire.[30] It was stowed carefully aboard, and the *Antelope* set sail again on 15 September 1666.

Almost a year later on 19 August 1667, the *Antelope* returned. From the proceeds of the sale of the linen, the agent had bought sugar for sale in England, and by the time the accounts were settled on 1 November, most of it had been sold. Blundell received £83 8s 6d, as well as his share of the one butt remaining unsold,[31] and a share of about 1,300 lb of

sugar that had been left behind in Barbados because there was no room
for it in the ship's hold. Six months later, Blundell received over £3 more
as the final accounts were settled, but whether that included the sugar
that had been left in Barbados, we cannot be sure. Certainly, he recorded
in his diary that he had 'cleared all with [his] ... sister', and he had made
over 200 per cent profit from his initial investment. Despite all the risks
and dangers, the whole venture had been most successful.[32]

When several other wealthy gentlemen, including the Norrises of
Speke Hall, heard about the successful voyage of the *Antelope*, they
too decided to invest in the West Indian trade, and in 1669, two other
ships, the *Lamb* and the *Providence*, left Liverpool. However, these early
voyages were not without risk, and shortly after Blundell's successful
venture, one Liverpool ship laden with sugar was taken by pirates and
all the merchants' investments were lost. By this time, the roles of a
century earlier had been reversed, the English were no longer the pirates,
but the victims of piracy. Nevertheless, the huge profits engendered by
a successful voyage made the ventures worthwhile, and by 1679, six
Liverpool ships were trading regularly with Barbados. The numbers
continued to increase,[33] boosting the quantity of sugar imported into
England until by 1700, the total amount of sugar imported in all the
ports of the country had risen to over 370,000 cwt, whereas in the
1660s, that total had been only 150,000 cwt.[34]

When William Stout, the Quaker merchant and diarist of Lancaster, heard
reports of several successful voyages to the West Indies from his home port,
he considered investing in importing sugar. He finally decided to participate
in the trade when he heard that the voyage of a ship financed by John
Hodgson of Lancaster yielded the immense profit of £1,500 in 1689.[35] He
agreed to become joint owner with two other Quakers, Robert Lawson and
Joshua Lawson, and four other Lancaster merchants, of the *Imployment*, a
ship of 70 tons built at Warton in 1698. They loaded the ship with various
provisions and goods for sale at the destination, and Stout's transatlantic
trading ventures began. Between 1699 and 1700, the ship made several
voyages – one to Virginia and two to Barbados, and then in 1701, it carried
a cargo to Norway, but none of these voyages proved to be very profitable
for the syndicate. Then in 1702, the ship again set sail again for Barbados,
and Stout and his associates hoped that this time they would recoup some
of their earlier losses. The *Imployment* arrived safely, and after the master

John Gardner had sold the cargo in Barbados, he loaded the ship with sugar, molasses, and ginger and set sail again for England. He sailed in convoy with several other ships in order to guard against attacks from the French, who were at war with the English at that time.

Unfortunately for the investors, the *Imployment* became separated from the rest of the convoy and was captured by the French, who demanded a ransom of £1,100 for its release. The master offered bravely to go with the French as their hostage if they would allow the ship to continue her voyage in the care of the mate. It was agreed that the master would remain a prisoner until the ransom had been paid, and the *Imployment* continued on her way. However, the mate, who according to Stout was not an experienced pilot, mistook the course into Lancaster and the ship ran aground at Rossall Point. A gale blew up and the ship was battered onto the shore. She began to fill with water rapidly and the crew decided that there was nothing they could do to save her, so they abandoned the ship and struggled ashore. As soon as they reached land, they sent a message to the owners in Lancaster, who immediately dispatched horses and carts to rescue as much of the cargo as possible. Fortunately, low tides followed the gale and it was possible to salvage most of the cargo. Attempts were then made to repair the ship, but the gales returned, forcing the carpenters to abandon the wreck and leave it to break up in the waves. The salvaged cargo, together with some of the rigging and those parts of the ship that had been saved from the wreck, were sold at auction. When the French heard what had happened to the ship, they agreed to reduce the ransom, and accepted £550 to release the master. Although Stout reckoned he had lost over £300 in the disaster, it did not prevent him from continuing to trade with the West Indies, which must have proved very lucrative for him despite all his misgivings.[36]

In 1713, the Treaty of Utrecht resulted in a large increase in English trade with the West Indies, for Britain was granted the contract to supply slaves to Spain's American colonies to work on both the sugar and the tobacco plantations. Therefore, more ships were needed to carry these slaves, and consequently, an increased number of ships were available to carry sugar, tobacco, and rum on their return voyage to Britain, resulting in more trade for the refiners.

Although the treaty had removed the threat from enemy ships on the high seas, it was still extremely perilous to trade with the West Indies. In the 1740s, Joshua Lawson of Lancaster, the master of a 70-ton vessel, was shipwrecked on the Welsh coast and wrote a letter describing his experience. A fierce gale tore the sails from the ship and she was driven against the rocks. The sailors managed to manoeuvre the ship back into the open sea, but without sails they were powerless to control her. They were driven back into another bay, where they found calmer waters and dropped anchor. Suddenly the local inhabitants appeared, swarmed aboard, broke open the hatches, and carried away the cargo of rum, sugar, and cotton. Not content with their booty, they returned and robbed the crew of all their money, and even took their clothes before breaking up the ship and carrying away as much of the timber as possible. The crew was extremely lucky to escape with their lives.[37]

During the Seven Years War (1756-1763), ships from the warring countries took every opportunity to attack each other, and consequently measures were taken by the British to protect their West Indian trade. Certain merchant ships known as privateers were equipped with guns to defend themselves, and also to protect any unarmed ships that were sailing in convoy with them. The Government licensed the privateers to attack and capture ships belonging to the enemy countries if the opportunity arose. One of these privateers was Captain Hutchinson of Liverpool, who thus had the chance to attack any French ship that was engaged in trade with the Indies. His success was recorded indirectly in an advertisement in the *Liverpool Courier* on 9 September 1757. The newspaper announced the sale of, 'The entire cargo of *Le Grand Marquis de Tournay*, Francis Delmas late Master, a French prize from St Domingo, taken by the Liverpool Privateer Capt. William Hutchinson Commander.' The Liverpool captain had scored a minor victory against the French when he captured of *Le Grand Marquis de Tournay*.[38]

After the cargo had been unloaded and examined, it was to be auctioned in Liverpool, and evidently, the auctioneer thought that the fact that the cargo had been captured from the French would act as an incentive to attract buyers to his sale. According to the advertisement, samples of the sugar, coffee, indigo, hides, and log wood from the cargo were also available for inspection in London, to assure prospective buyers that they had not been damaged either by fire or water during the attack or the capture of the vessel. The auctioneer chose to sell the cargo 'by candle', and so to excite more interest in the sale by introducing an

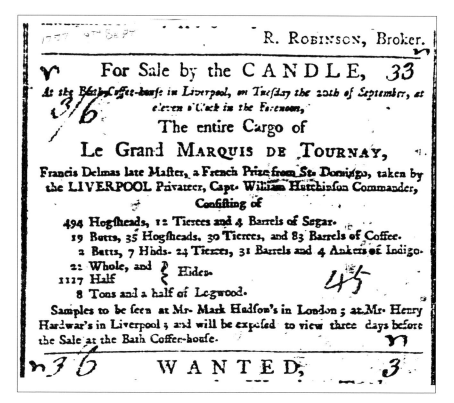

From the *Liverpool Courier* issued on 9 September 1757. (*Reproduced by kind permission of Liverpool Record Office*)

element of chance into the proceedings. A small piece of candle was lit, and the bidder whose bid was made immediately before the candle went out, or before it burned down to a pin placed 1 inch from the top of the candle, was the successful bidder. It is significant that this advertisement was intended for the eyes of merchants and sugar boilers in London, thus providing evidence that traders in the capital were taking a serious interest in sugar sales in Liverpool. In fact, this sale could be interpreted as a sign that by 1757, Liverpool was challenging London's position as the centre of the English sugar trade.

The cargo of *Le Grand Marquis de Tournay* consisted mainly of hogsheads of sugar – 494 in all – together with smaller quantities of sugar – all carefully listed – and also, as we saw, coffee, indigo, hides, and log wood – presumably hardwood for the furniture industry. This list has a significant parallel in the inventory of James Berry, a grocer

Part of the inventory of James Berry listing among his possessions his stock of sugar. (*Reproduced by kind permission of Lancashire Record Office*)

from Ormskirk, that was compiled in 1686.[39] When he died, the goods in his shop were valued and listed in an inventory. Among his stock was 28 lb of Barbados sugar at 6s (this price suggests that the sugar was brown sugar that had not been refined), 2 cwt bottoms of casks of Barbados sugar worth £1 16s, various other types of sugar, 16 lb of Barbados indigo valued at £2 8s, 40 cwt of log wood worth 8s 4d, and a range of spices.

Evidently, long before the capture of *Le Grand Marquis*, this grocer in the small market town in south west Lancashire had been supplied with a range of similar goods by merchants trading with Barbados, and those who valued his stock after his death knew exactly where the goods had been produced. It is surprising how quickly a trade in West Indian goods had been established in the hinterland of Lancashire, especially when it is remembered that Barbados was captured in 1625, and that it was almost twenty years before the production of sugar was established.[40]

The hides and log wood in *Le Grand Marquis* would have been packed around the hogsheads of sugar in the hold of the ship. Possibly they had been stacked at the quayside in Barbados, waiting to be included in any

A brigantine and a snow.

cargo for Europe that had space available for them. The agents who organised the transport of these non-perishable goods were confident that there would be a ready market for them whenever the ship arrived in its European port. In fact, log wood became a major import from the West Indies to Lancaster once Gillows the furniture manufacturers were established in 1729.

On 17 November 1758, there was yet another sale of casks of French prize sugar and bags of French colonial coffee at the Merchants' Coffee House in Liverpool – a tavern on the south-west corner of the churchyard of St Nicholas Church. Again, both the coffee and the sugar had been captured from a French ship, and prospective buyers were advised that they could see samples of both products by applying to the broker or agent.

The advertisement for this sale also included a notice that the snow *Lovely Martha* was to be sold immediately after the sale of the cargo. A snow was a sailing ship of about 20 to 30 tons, between 40 and 50 feet long. These ships, together with brigantines – similar ships with different rigging – were the vessels that were used for the slave trade, for they needed only a small number of sailors to control them, and so could carry a large human cargo. Although ships were often sold when they docked in Liverpool, the inclusion of the snow in this advertisement for the sale of her cargo suggests that the *Lovely Martha* had been involved

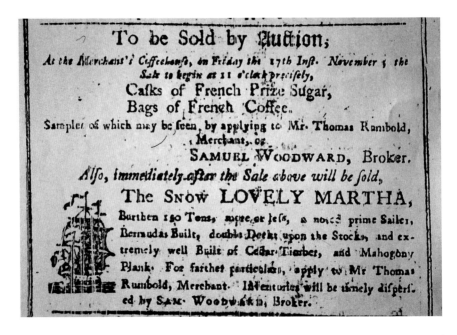

The advertisement for the auction 10 November 1758. (*Reproduced by kind permission of Liverpool Record Office*)

The advertisement for freight or passengers for the *Bolden* in the *Liverpool Chronicle* 7 January 1768. (*Reproduced by kind permission of Liverpool Record Office*)

in capturing the booty from the French. It is possible that the owner wanted to sell her because she had been damaged in the engagement, making her unfit for the West Indian trade, although considered her fit for coastal trading.

Another snow, the *Mary*, was also to be sold, but this time it was mentioned specifically that the ship had arrived recently from Tortola in the West Indies. It was being sold by John Tarleton, the Liverpool merchant and sugar refiner, the history of whose sugar house will be examined later.[41] The *Bolden* was the subject of yet another advertisement in January 1768, in which her master William Priestman appealed for both freight and passengers for her voyage to the James River in Virginia. However, included in this sale were twenty-five hogsheads of fine Barbados sugar – no doubt the previous cargo of the *Bolden* on its return run from Barbados. Here we find a ship involved in trade with both Virginia and Barbados, a common extension of the 'triangular' trade.[42]

Thus sugar cane was processed and imported into the North West in the seventeenth and eighteenth centuries. The next stage of its journey involved various towns in Lancashire, Cheshire, and Cumberland, and we now turn to examine the establishment of refineries in these centres.

CHAPTER 2

The Liverpool Refineries

Unlikely though it may seem, Liverpool's sugar refining industry owes its origins to the great fire of London, for it was that tragedy that compelled Alleyn Smith of Battersea to relocate his business. Smith was one of the capital's leading sugar refiners, and was extremely wealthy, being worth £40,000 in the 1660s according to a report received by Sir Edward Moore of Liverpool at that time.[43] Nevertheless, as a result of the plague, the profits of his sugar house in London had been decimated Then, when the fire struck, his business in the capital was destroyed. As Pepys reported shortly afterwards, 'The houses too (were) so very thick thereabouts and full of matter for burning, as pitch and tar and warehouses of oyle and wines, and brandy and other things.'[44]Among those 'other things' was Alleyn Smith's stock of sugar. Any butts of sugar that were not completely destroyed by the fire were lost in the pillaging and looting that followed it. Again, Pepys described the scene as women tried to clean up after the fire: 'It was pretty to see how hard the women did work in the cannells sweeping of water, but then they would scold for drink, and be as drunk as devils. I saw good butts of sugar broke open in the street and people give and take handfuls out and put into beer and drink it.'[45]

After the tragedy, Smith decided to look elsewhere for a site for a new sugar refinery. Many factors had to be considered. Would there be a source of fuel nearby to heat the boilers? How near was a river for the shipping to deliver the raw sugar, and would there be a plentiful supply of labour? If he found a satisfactory position, would the land be available for the building? Liverpool, where at that time the merchants were developing trade with the West Indies, was near the Lancashire coal fields and had a suitable labour force. In fact, Liverpool's population was increasing rapidly, so much so that between 1660 and 1708, it had expanded from 1,500 to 6,000.[46] An available work force would be no problem. Also the wages in the North West were highly favourable, being between a third and a half of those paid in London.[47] The port met all his requirements, so with these facts in mind, Smith approached one of the leading landowners of the town, Sir Edward Moore of Bank Hall.

Sir Edward recorded the results of that meeting in a memorandum to his son (written 1666-1667) observing that 'Mr Smith, a great sugar baker at London ... came from London to treat with me'. The negotiations were successful, and even the finer details of the plan had been decided. As Sir Edward reported:

According to agreement, he is to build all the front 27 yards, a stately house of good hewn stone four stories high and then to go through the house with a large entry and there on the back side, to erect a house for boiling and drying sugar, otherwise called a sugar baker's house. The pile of building must be 40 foot square and four stories high all of hewn stone; then he is to take the little [house] of Richard Rogerson in Dig Lane and make the back way in through there; then he is to encompass all his ground with a brick wall round.

Sir Edward commented, 'If this be once done, it will bring a trade of at least £40,000 a year from the Barbados, which formerly this town never knew.[48]

Sir Edward's pleasure at the prospect of increased income for the town was not completely altruistic, for he also advised his son that, as the house would cost at least £1,400, it would be worth £50 a year in rent for himself and his heirs – an extremely good investment for the future. He also told his son to negotiate a yearly rental rather than leasing it for a long term, then presumably, he would be able to increase the rent if the sugar house proved very profitable. Sir Edward was so enthusiastic about the proposition that he renamed the plot of land 'on the left hand of the Dale Street as you go out of the town almost over against Mr Olive's house', Sugar House Close. However, his optimism for the outcome of

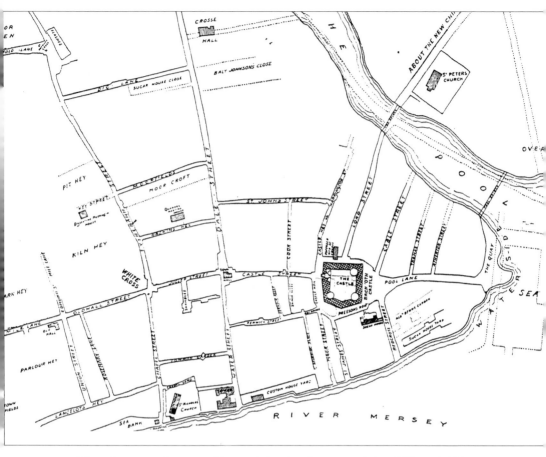

Map of seventeenth-century Liverpool showing the proposed site of Alleyn Smith's sugar house. (*Reproduced by kind permission of Liverpool Record Office*)

the talks must have been short-lived, for it is doubtful whether Alleyn Smith ever built his sugar refinery on Sugar House Close. If he did, he soon abandoned the project and chose a new site for his refinery in Red Cross Street, nearer to the River Mersey, a much more convenient site for the transfer of barrels of sugar from the quayside to the refinery.[49]

In 1670, Smith appointed his twenty-six year old brother-in-law Daniel Danvers[50] to be a partner in the business in Red Cross Street, together with Richard Cleveland, who had married Daniel's sister Susanna. Thus, although the different surnames suggest otherwise, the first sugar refinery in Liverpool was indeed a family business. In fact, the relationships were even more interwoven, for Daniel's elder brother

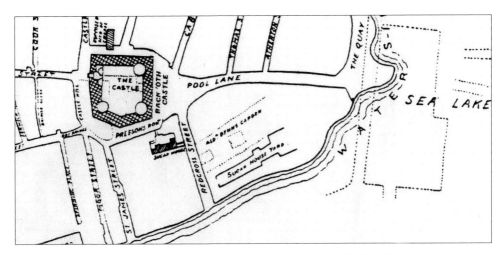

A map of the actual site of the sugar house complex that was developed by Danvers.

John had been involved in Smith's sugar boiling business in London. This suggests that Daniel too may have been trained in the trade, or at least have had some experience of it, before coming to Liverpool.

Soon afterwards in 1682, an incident occurred that suggests a link in the religious beliefs, and possibly, some commercial collaboration between the early refiners in Liverpool and other sugar boilers in the North West. During that year, both Cleveland and Danvers were summoned to the Consistory Court in Chester to answer the charge that they had not attended any services in the local church. The two sugar refiners ignored the summons, and consequently, the court excommunicated them for forty days. When they eventually did appear before the court, they were sentenced to enter a bond for £20 each to promise to attend the church. Sureties were given by Nicholas Johnson, a soap boiler of Chester, and Thomas Buck, a grocer from Chester, both of whom were known to the two sugar refiners.[51] This suggests that all of them were dissenters who did not agree with the teachings of the established Church. A dissenters' chapel was built in the centre of the sugar house complex, so the family must have agreed to it and possibly worshipped there. The early sugar refiners in Chester were also dissenters, while most of the refiners in Lancaster were Quakers, who also did not worship in the established Church. Whether this connection between those of a similar religious persuasion was exploited in their commercial dealings is difficult to

Red Cross Street as it was in the eighteenth century. The street was named after a red sandstone cross that stood nearby and was the site of an early market. It is possible that the archway led into the sugar house complex. (*Reproduced from a painting by W. G. Herdman by courtesy of the Athenaeum Club*)

The modern law courts at the rear of the memorial were built on the site of Danvers' first sugar house complex on Red Cross Street.

Lord Street in late eighteenth century. The four-storey building on the right was probably Danvers' second sugar house. (*Reproduced from a painting by W. G. Herdman by courtesy of the Athenaeum Club*)

prove, but it is extremely likely. This case is also interesting in the context of the development of Liverpool, because that chapel was the first to be built by dissenters in the town.

If they were not already acting as merchants, many refiners extended their interests in the sugar trade by acting in that capacity. Daniel Danvers senior diversified in this way; in fact in 1692, he was involved in a court case at the Chancery Court, concerning a quantity of oats that he had supplied. The customer complained that they were 'black oats' from Wales, and not the superior oats from Lancashire that he had ordered.[52] Danvers also had an interest in a distillery in Church Gate, Bolton, which is mentioned in his will of 1709/10. No doubt the molasses extracted at his refinery in Liverpool would have been used to produce rum in that distillery. Eventually, the Danvers family's involvement in the sugar industry extended to the West Indies in 1729, when Daniel's son John, usually described as a merchant, proved his right to a sugar refining business in Jamaica. His other son Anthony, also a merchant dealing mainly in sugar, became the assay master in Jamaica in 1764.

The refinery in Red Cross Street must have proved very profitable, because sometime about the turn of the century, Danvers opened a second refinery in Lord Street in Liverpool. It first appears in the records in 1705, when Danvers was assessed by the council for 10s 6d in rates for the sugar house and an empty house on the same site. However, the fact that the house was empty is very significant, for if the refinery had been in full operation at that time, the house would have been occupied by one of the workers. In fact, three years later, according to the rate book for 1708, that sugar house had been sold to John Tatlock and was described as 'the old sugar house'. Together with two houses, it was assessed for 12s – a very low assessment for a thriving sugar house and two occupied houses. This suggests that the new refinery had not been as successful as Danvers had hoped, and so he had sold it to Tatlock. As neither Tatlock nor his tenant, a Mr Cunningham, appear in any documents as sugar bakers, that trade must have been abandoned and the building in Lord Street put to some other use.[53]

After Daniel Danvers death, the sugar refinery in Red Cross Street became the property of another son, Samuel, who outlived his father by only ten years. In his will, there is a detailed description of the sugar house and the surrounding property, which belonged to the family in Red Cross Street (now the site of the law courts).[54] The sugar industry involved many other dependent industries or crafts, and it was much more convenient if all these different trades operated in the same locality. Consequently, the sugar house complex in Red Cross Street included a warehouse, a stable, and a cooperage – a cooper's workshop – as well as the actual sugar boiling house. Also on the site was the 'distil house', where rum was produced from the molasses extracted from the raw sugar during the refining process. The complex also included a hen house and a swine yard, buildings which we would consider more appropriate for a rural location than for an industrial site within a few hundred yards of the Liverpool quayside. However, it would seem that the hens and pigs were fed on the waste products from the refining process, while the eggs, chickens, bacon, and pork were consumed by the family and by the workers who lived in the same complex.

Also on the family's land in Red Cross Street was a pair of adjoining houses, which Samuel left to his wife Isabel,[55] while his brother Daniel inherited another large house in Red Cross Street, which had been

Samuel's home before he died. Behind the two adjoining houses was a large garden, about 94 yards long, and a summer house. It is difficult nowadays to envisage a garden in such close proximity to an industrial complex, but it seems to have been customary at that time, even though the constant smoke from the boilers must have polluted the air, and the noise of the continual activity must have disturbed the tranquillity of the garden.[56] It is possible that Samuel had aspirations to build a large house in the country, for he owned land on the Wirral, 'on the road from Liverpool to Parkgate', but nothing had been done with the land at the time of his death. He also had properties in Tithebarn Street in Liverpool, which might have been built on part of the original Sugar House Close, the subject of negotiations fifty years earlier with Sir Edward Moore, but that is difficult to prove. These properties were divided between his other brothers and sisters, while his brother Daniel continued as a partner in the Liverpool business until his death in 1745, when yet another Daniel Danvers took possession of the refinery.

Tragedy struck the firm five years later, when a fire broke out in Danvers' first sugar house, according to the *Weekly Courant* of Chester on 13 November 1750. This reference to the first sugar house suggests that the partnership had erected a second building, or possibly the report excluded the new extension that was mentioned in Samuel's will. However, as almost forty years had passed since Samuel's death, it is likely that a completely new boiling house had been built in the interim. The *Weekly Courant* reported, 'Last Monday night about eleven o'clock, a fire broke out at the sugar house in Liverpool, which burnt with such violence that in a short space the building was entirely consumed, it being a rejoicing day the men had left off work at three o'clock, and it is conjectured, had not taken proper care of the stoves.'[57]

However, the Danvers family's connection with sugar refining in Liverpool did not end with the fire. They must have rebuilt the refinery and continued in business. It was not until 1758, eight years after the fire, that they finally sold the sugar house in Red Cross Street, after almost ninety years in the trade. In the advertisement, it was described as being in Crooked Lane, the road on the other side of the same complex. On 9 June 1758, the Liverpool paper had this advertisement:

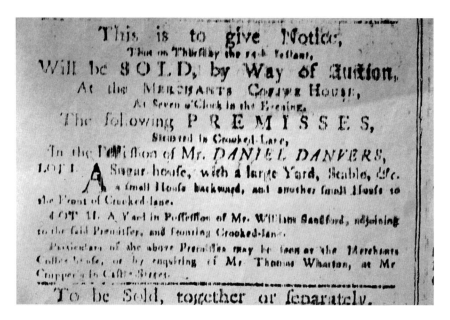

The newspaper advertisement.

This is to give Notice

That on Thursday the 14 Instant

Will be SOLD, by Way of Auction,

At the Merchant's Coffee House,

At Seven o'clock in the Evening

The following PREMISES

Situated in Crooked Lane

In the Possession of Mr. Daniel Danvers

Lot I. A Sugar house, with a large Yard, Stable etc.

A small House backward, and another small House to

the Front of Crooked Lane

Lot II A Yard in Possession of Mr William Sandford, adjoining

to the said Premises and fronting Crooked Lane

Particulars of the above Premises may be seen at the Merchants'

Coffee house or by enquiring of Mr Thomas Wharton at Mr

Cropper in Castle Street

The outcome the sale is not reported, but in 1762, it was recorded that Isaac Oldham leased the Red Cross Street sugar house. Then in 1766, when the Liverpool Directory listed the chief businesses of the town, it included the sugar house in Red Cross Street as belonging to Caldwell and Oldham. It also listed another company belonging to Thomas Wakefield as sugar refiners at the same address in Red Cross Street. It is possible that Danvers' original business had been divided into two different operations, but that seems unlikely. As Caldwell and Oldham do not appear to have continued in business after that date, the more likely explanation is that Thomas Wakefield & Company were in the process of taking over the concern when the directory was being compiled. Consequently, the publishers decided to include both firms among the eight sugar boilers in Liverpool. Certainly, Oldham must have sold his shares in the sugar house shortly afterwards and invested elsewhere, for when he died in 1782, he left a large quantity of stocks and shares, none of which had any connection with sugar refining.[58]

Later, Wakefield's company was converted into a partnership with Okill, and that firm continued operating until the death of Wakefield in 1770. Wakefield was a shrewd business man, for in his will he left instructions that 'none of my children shall be paid their fortune ... till such time as the present Sugar House partnership expires, which is about nine years to come'. He inserted this clause to safeguard the immediate future of the refinery, by ensuring that the executors would not be forced to sell his shareholding in order to pay out the beneficiaries. That objective was achieved, and the company continued satisfactorily until the 1780s, when the partnership was extended to include William Skelhorne.

This partnership was short lived, and it seems possible that Skelhorne had joined the partnership only in order to learn about the business, or perhaps to indulge in some industrial espionage. Certainly by 1789, he had formed his own company, trading as William Skelhorne & Co., and was in competition with his earlier partnership. This company was based in Castle Street, where it had leased the refinery from the Tarleton family. When Skelhorne died in 1789, he left instructions that his wife and eldest son should carry on the business 'with the assistance of good clerks', because he considered that it would 'be of advantage' to his family.[59] This was done, and in the 1790 directory William Skelhorne – presumably the eldest son – was described as a sugar baker in business in Castle Street.

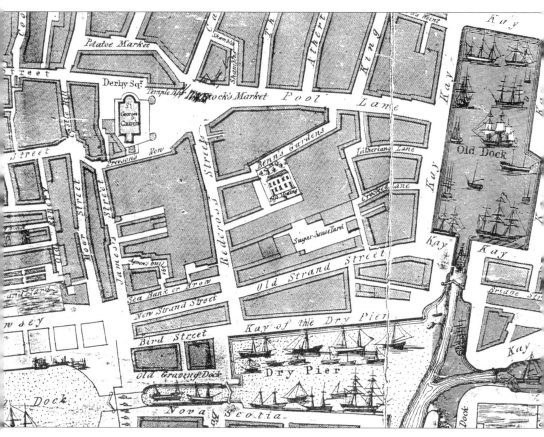

Part of Eyes map of 1765 showing the location of the Red Cross Street sugar house, the Dissenters' meeting house and St George's church. (*Reproduced by kind permission of Liverpool Record Office*)

Meanwhile, the firm of Wakefield and Okill continued until 1799 in Danvers' sugar house, then described as being in Preeson's Row, St George's. Of course by this time, St George's Church had been built on the site of the castle behind the sugar house complex. It is interesting that, when plans were being made for the church in 1702, a letter was written to Richard Norris by Thomas Johnson from London, suggesting 'that a handsome plan be drawn, and that the side next the sugar house be made the front – that is taking it from Mr. Danvers' garden wall to the farthest extent towards Poole Lane'.[60] Evidently, it was not considered that the proximity of the industrial site would detract from the front elevation of the church.

However, tragedy struck again in May of that year, and the old work place of the Danvers family, the Caldwell and Oldham partnership, and finally of the Wakefield and Okill partnership, was destroyed. As *Billinge's Liverpool Advertiser* for Monday 27 May 1799 reported:

> On Wednesday night last, the Sugar House near St George's church belonging to Messrs Wakefield and Okill was entirely consumed by fire. It broke out about eight o'clock and by ten, the building was a mere shell. The appearance was truly alarming and dreadful! From the great exertion and activity of all ranks, the fire was kept from spreading to the adjoining houses, though we are apprehensive some of the neighbours must suffer considerably.

The newspaper continued to praise the efforts of all concerned in the incident in the days before fire brigades and salvage teams existed, and provided a valuable eye witness's account of the scene:

> In all cases of emergency here, we have to notice the alacrity with which all ranks and different sorts of persons step forth to render their assistance, and it was with particular satisfaction we observed on the unhappy occasion of the dreadful fire at the sugar refinery of Messrs Wakefield and Okill not only the spirited activity of the regular forces, but the early appearance on the spot of the Picquet Guard of the Royal Liverpool Regiment of Volunteers, who placed themselves under the temporary command of Major Bromley of the Worcestershire Provisional Cavalry, the field officer of the day, and remained on duty the whole night as well to six o'clock next morning co-operating with the troops of the garrison in preserving order and protecting property, indeed too much praise cannot be given to the whole regiment who attended and volunteered to relieve those, whose lot it had fallen to be the first on duty.

Another sugar refinery founded early in the eighteenth century was that of Rauthmell and Gildart in Harrington Street. This time, it was not the result of a need to relocate, but as a response to the increasing trade with the West Indies, and later, to the development of Liverpool docks. In contrast to the Danvers family, both partners were already merchants when the deed of partnership was drawn up. Evidently, they envisaged

St George's Church. The sugar house can be seen in the shadow behind the church. Queen Victoria's monument stands on the site of the church today.

the sugar refinery as a profitable extension to their trading concerns with the West Indies, rather than as a completely new independent venture.

Little has been recorded about Henry Rauthmell, although we know that his partner James Gildart was a member of a long established Liverpool merchant family. They were part of the mercantile oligarchy, which dominated the town council after the grant of the new charter was confirmed in 1695. James' father, Richard Gildart the elder, had served as mayor, and James' brother, also called Richard, was elected to be the Member of Parliament for Liverpool in 1734, 1741, and 1747.[61] James himself had served as a member of the council for many years, and was mayor in 1750. They, like Alleyn Smith of the Red Cross Street refinery, also negotiated with the Moore family with a view to buying a portion of the Moore's estate, and in 1709, Richard completed a deal to purchase some land north of the town near Bevington Hill. However that land, like Danvers' Sugar House Close, did not become the site of a sugar refinery, and later became known as Gildart's Gardens.[62]

During the early years of the eighteenth century, Liverpool council became involved in a far-sighted and very expensive undertaking. They commissioned Thomas Steers to construct their first dock in 1715, and followed that with a second, the Salthouse Dock in 1738.[63] Consequently, they were very keen to increase the use made of the docks, and also the income generated by them, by encouraging the development of industries that would utilise the docks for the import of their raw materials. The Gildart family, as members of the council, had supported this initiative, and so extended their trading interests to include sugar refining, an industry that certainly made use of the new docks. Of course, they benefited from the new facilities that made it much easier to import and transfer great quantities of hogsheads (large barrels) of partially refined sugar to their new sugar house.

The family used the new docks for a very different purpose in the years of 1746-47, when Alderman Richard Gildart won a Government contract, whereby Jacobite prisoners would be transported across the Atlantic to the sugar plantations. At that time, the Government was embarrassed by the large number of prisoners, who had been found guilty of treason after the Jacobite rebellion of 1745. According to legislation passed in 1617, the Crown could hand prisoners over to contractors for deportation to the American colonies. The Jacobite prisoners were

The side of an old building in
Harrington Street. It may have been
the wall of the original sugar house.
Certainly it is constructed of handmade
bricks which were revealed when the
neighbouring property was demolished.

given the opportunity to choose deportation instead of hanging, on
condition that they confessed that they had been guilty of treason. The
orders in council were read to them, and then they signed a petition for
transportation. The women and children among the prisoners were given
the first chance, and then lots were drawn as to which prisoners could
choose to be sent to the plantations. Once they reached the plantations,
they would serve as indented servants – virtually slaves – for seven years,
and then they would be freed. Richard Gildart, who had some previous
experience of transporting human cargoes from Africa to the sugar
fields, agreed to act as the contractor to take 936 women and children
across the Atlantic at the cost to the Government of £5 each. Once they
arrived, they were to be treated as his property, and he intended to sell
their indentures for £7 each. Thus, Richard stood to make £12 for each
servant he transported.

The plan seemed foolproof to the family. However, unlike his usual
cargoes, the prisoners were not congregated on the docks awaiting
transport, but were housed in many different jails up and down the
country. In fact, it was not until 1747 that they were all assembled in
Liverpool. Meanwhile, some had been living in terrible conditions in

Richard Gildart (1673-1770) son of James Gildart and
Elizabeth Sweeting of Middleham Freeman 1698, Bailiff
1712, Mayor 1714-15 MP 1735-54. (*Photograph of a
portrait by Joseph Wright of c. 1745. Reproduced by
courtesy of the Athenaeum Club*)

tiny town jails, while others had been shackled in the holds of various
hulks in Liverpool docks awaiting the arrival of those who had been
imprisoned temporarily in more distant places. Gildart became very
concerned about his cargo. He feared that he would lose his investment
if the prisoners' departure was delayed any longer and they died of
fever. Indeed he did lose several who were drowned when they were
being transferred to a large sea-going ship moored mid-Mersey. Their
small boat sank after striking a rope hawser, and they had no chance
of surviving because they were shackled with heavy iron leg irons. As
a result of that incident, Gildart wrote to the treasury asking for £40
compensation for his losses. He claimed that he had paid for bedding
and provisions for the prisoners' passage across the Atlantic and they
would not be needed. Finally in late May the *Gildart*, with eighty-seven
prisoners cramped in its hold, set sail in convoy with other hell ships for
the Caribbean.[64]

While these events were taking place, James Gildart was involved in
negotiations with his partners to set up a new sugar house in Liverpool.
The partnership agreement involving James Gildart, and the early deeds
of the property that was destined to become the Rauthmell and Gildart's
sugar refinery, still exist.[65] Therefore, the history of the transfer of the
land on which the sugar house was eventually built can be traced from
as early as 1682. In fact, these transfers chart the early development and

expansion of Liverpool, as the Atlantic trade brought more economic opportunities to the town. In 1682, John Harrington, whose land extended from the castle to the pool,[66] leased some of his land for development to Richard Moorcroft, and a few years later he released more, and granted leases for new cottages to various tenants, including a shoemaker and a tanner. Meanwhile, in 1692, Peter Rainford, an astute entrepreneur foreseeing the future development of the town, leased part of Moorcroft's land, and also acquired more land from Harrington. He consolidated his holding in 1711, when he obtained leases for more houses from Harrington's trustees. Several of the names of these early landowners and developers can be traced in the modern street names. In fact, as early as 1711, we find references to Harrington Street, and the map of 1765 shows Rainford's gardens adjoining it. Another early landowner who is commemorated in a street name was Matthew Plunkington, who owned the strip of land adjoining that of Harrington. Part of his land was developed into Plunkington's Alley, later to become Matthew Street – well known for its modern connections with the Beatles and the Cavern Club.[67]

After many years of acquiring different plots of land, Peter Rainford – an alderman by this time – finally consolidated a site large enough for a sugar house, and began to build a complex for that purpose. By 1746, Rainford had erected several buildings, including a sugar house, a warehouse, stables, and several other buildings on a piece of land, measuring 34 yards by 18 yards, between Harrington Street and Pluckington's Alley. Then once it was completed, he leased it to a partnership, who agreed to pay £3 17s 7d rent twice a year for twenty-one years. The partners included Thomas Greenup,[68] Thomas Bell, James Gildart, and Richard Cribb, all of whom were prominent Liverpool merchants with an interest in the West Indian trade, and who agreed to trade under the name of Cribb & Co.

Although this firm operated successfully for several years, few records exist about their business. However, they are recorded as the custodians of the local fire engine. As we have seen, sugar refineries were very vulnerable to fire, mainly because of the inflammable nature of the sugar. The threat was increased by the open fires that burned under the stoves where the sugar was boiled. Consequently, the parish authorities took great precautions to prevent any fires from spreading from the refineries, and possibly affecting the whole town.[69] They had already invested in a fire engine – virtually a tank on wheels with a simple manual pumping mechanism – very different to today's sophisticated machines. After the disaster at Danvers' sugar house in 1750, the Liverpool vestry decided that the best place to keep their fire engine was as close as possible to the most likely source of another fire. That would be in the grounds of a sugar house, so they rented a space in Cribb & Co.'s warehouse. However, difficulties of some kind arose, and the members of the vestry decided to move the engine to another sugar house in the vicinity, belonging to Knight & Co. The vestry book of 1754 records that decision, 'Ordered that the parish engine, which is kept at Mr Cribb's warehouse in Castle Hey, be

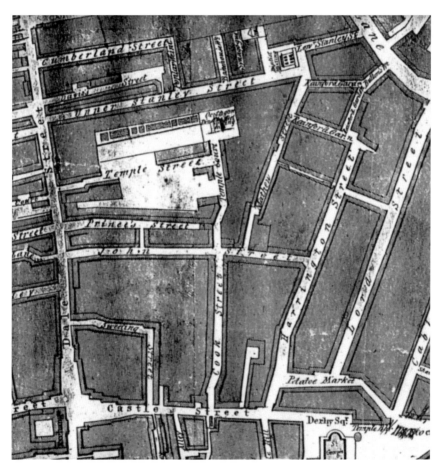

A section of Eyes map of 1765 showing the location of Rauthmell and Gildart's refinery between Harrington Street and Matthew Street.

Matthew Street today, the site of Cribb's refinery.

on account of the inconvenient situation, removed to a shed belonging to Mr Knight & Co. at their sugar house in Castle Hey, they making the said shed doors to the said street and to be allowed the present rent.'[70]

After Richard Cribb's death in 1755,[71] a new partnership agreement had to be drawn up to incorporate four new partners: William Gregson, John Bridge, and John Walker all Liverpool merchants, and also John Baicklin, a sugar baker of Liverpool, who evidently was included because of his experience in the trade. Although there is no mention of the nationality of this last partner, his unusual surname suggests that he may have come from the Low Countries. As we have seen, the early development of sugar plantations in the Dutch South American colonies had meant that both Amsterdam and Antwerp were well-established centres of sugar refining at that time. Consequently, it is possible that Baicklin came from one of those cities, where he had been trained in

Castle Hey – Present day Harrington Street, the site of Knight's refinery.

his trade. Alternatively he may have been one of the first of the many German sugar boilers, who later joined the work forces of the various sugar refineries in Liverpool. In the contract dated 1757, the partners agreed to trade under the name of Rauthmell, Gildart & Company as 'joint traders in the art, trade, mystery, and business of sugar bakers' for the next twenty-one years.[72] The premises were described as being in Rainford Square,[73] and an inventory was made of all the various possessions of the partnership, including the utensils of the trade and all the different properties in the complex.[74] Twenty-four shares, each costing £100, were issued and divided among the partners: Gildart bought eight, Rauthmell five, Baicklin two shares, and the others had three each. This produced a working capital of £2,400.

The five other partners certainly valued Baicklin's expertise in boiling sugar, for they agreed to loan him the money for his shares. In return, he gave them a bond that he would repay the money with interest 'upon a reasonable demand made to him', while the other partners deducted £9 each year from of his salary as interest on the loan. He was given the responsibility of overseeing the actual process of boiling the sugar, and in return he was given:

> For his care and trouble therein, the yearly salary of £60 6s weekly as board wages and to have the dwelling house he now lives in rent-free, it being part of the estate of the said co-partnership, and also such quantity of coals and candles at the company's expense as shall be necessary and reasonable for the use of himself and family in his dwelling house only, and likewise to be at liberty to have and take to the private use of his own family only so much sugar out of the said company stock as they shall reasonably have occasion for during and so long as he shall act in the capacity of boiler of sugar aforesaid.

If the lawyers had defined exactly what was considered to be a reasonable amount of candles, coals and sugar at that date, it would have given us an interesting insight into the daily life of the sugar baker, but unfortunately, such detailed accounts are rarely given.

Meanwhile, in addition to being treasurer for the company, Henry Rauthmell was made manager, buyer, and salesman for the concern, and was given a salary of £100 per annum. No other partner was allowed to negotiate any deals without his consent, and he was to use one of the rooms in his own house as the accounting house. In return for accepting these responsibilities, he too was allowed as much sugar as he could 'reasonably have occasion for'. Even his competitors were forced to acknowledge that Rauthmell was an astute businessman. For instance in 1758, Joseph Manesty, a Liverpool merchant, wrote to his partner in the Chester sugar refinery about one of Rauthmell's successful deals. Manesty observed that the new Liverpool refinery had been very lucky to obtain raw sugar at the unusually low price of 34s to 37/6d per hogshead. Seemingly, Rauthmell had grasped the opportunity and had bought 600 hogsheads at that price.[75] Manesty regretted that he had missed his chance of a bargain, with grave consequences for the Chester refinery.

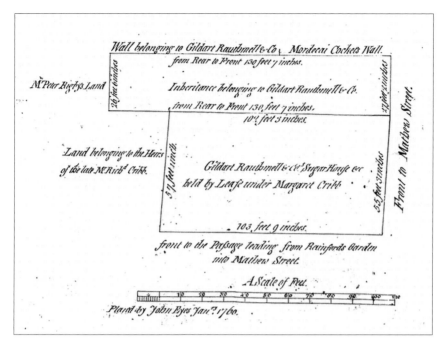

A plan of Gildart and Rauthmell's property as it was at the time of Cribb's death in 1755. (*Reproduced by kind permission of Arnold Greenwood, Solicitors, and the Cumbria Record Office [Kendal] Ref: WD/AG Box 1/8*)

Five years later in 1763, the partner John Bridge died, and bequeathed his shares in the sugar house to his son James,[76] a merchant who lived in Paradise Street. As well as being involved in sugar refining, John had continued to act as a merchant, and also had shares in a rope house and a pot house, all of which were left to James. This wide range of investments illustrate the seemingly diverse interests of a typical Liverpool businessman. In fact, all his interests were very closely interconnected. As a merchant, he bought and transported raw sugar, his rope works provided ropes for his sailing ships, warehouse hoists, and countless other uses, while his pot house provided moulds for the refining process.

Whether there was some disagreement between the partners, or whether the new partner had prompted a move to another location is unclear, but certainly in 1768, the decision was made to sell the sugar house in Matthew Street. An advertisement appeared in the local press describing the property involved in the sale, consisting of the sugar house,

A pottery on Shaw's Brow, the site of William Brown Street, possibly the pottery belonging to John Bridge. (*Reproduced from a painting by W. G. Herdman, courtesy of the Athenaeum Club*)

a warehouse, a counting house, a mill, stables, a cooperage, and four dwelling houses. The whole estate was still held under a lease from 'the late Mr Rainford', the builder of the complex. However, an extension to that lease had been granted when two of the original lives named in the 1746 lease had died, and the property was now held for two more lives. Two of the partners, Henry Rauthmell and John Baicklin, still occupied houses in the complex, so evidently, they too had no objection to living close to their work, despite all the noise and smoke generated by the refinery. Of course, the accounting house was probably still part of Rauthmell's residence, while Baicklin would have to live near his work as manager of the boiling process. The other two tenants were named as James Laithwaite, possibly the cooper employed in making and repairing barrels for the refined sugar,[77] and Samuel Appleton, described as a pork seller in the 1766 directory. What exactly happened at that sale is unclear, for the Rauthmell family were still involved in sugar refining in that area for at least another twenty years after the sale of these premises.

When Henry Rauthmell died in 1787, he left his shares to John Farrer on condition that he would relinquish them to Rauthmell's nephew Robert if he was alive at the time of his uncle's death.[78] Robert had not been in contact with the family for four years, so his uncle thought he must have died. Of course, it was possible that he had survived and merely lost contact with his relations. During the mid-eighteenth century, many members of the Rauthmell family had crossed the Atlantic to visit the plantations, or to oversee various transactions in connection with their roles as merchants. Life in the West Indies was fraught with danger, and travelling abroad in sailing ships at that time always involved a risk, and Henry suspected that Robert was one of the casualties. Certainly, he did not claim his legacy, so it would seem that indeed he had died abroad.

By the late 1780s, all the original partners had relinquished their shares, and the control of the business had passed into the hands of William Beckwith and William Farrer. It is recorded that James Gildart of Whiston died in 1790, leaving a vast amount of property, mainly coal mines and similar investments.[79] Whether he was the original partner in the sugar refinery who had left Liverpool and diversified, is hard to tell. However, his executor was William Gregson of Everton, possibly his ex-partner, which suggests that this was the original entrepreneur who had moved into other more profitable fields of investment. By 1790, William Beckwith had also left sugar refining, and had become a timber merchant with a yard and counting house. William Farrer had moved away to Preston, where he died in 1795.[80] As he left less than £300, he had not found wealth in his new home town. Even John Baichlin seems to have moved to pastures new, for in his will dated 1781, he was described as a plumber and glazier.[81]

Although all these moves would seem to spell the end of the old refinery, that was not to be. During the early 1790s, the refinery passed into the hands of Nicholas Distell, a sugar baker who was mentioned in the will of John Baicklin, and he continued working there for about twenty-five years. However, between 1794 and 1800, two other refiners, Stephen Waterworth and George Jagen, were also listed in the directories as operating in Rainford's Gardens and Harrington Street, the site of the Gildart and Rauthmell refinery. This suggests either that the refinery had been split up into three smaller firms, or more likely, that the three were partners in the one business. The refinery must have prospered during

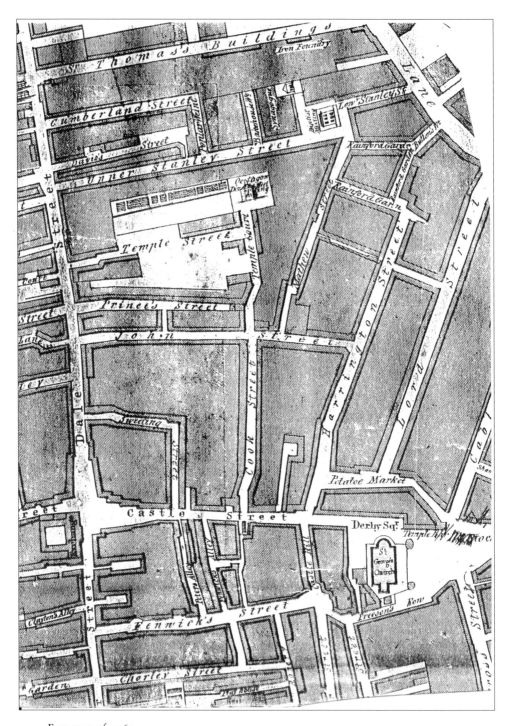

Eyes map of 1765.

Liverpool, September 28th, 1768.
To be Sold by Auction,
At the Sign of the Millstone in Castle-street, on Thursday the 20th of October, 1768.
THE SUGARHOUSE in Matthew-street, belonging to GILDART, RAUTHMELL, and Co. with all its Utensils, together with a Warehouse, Counting House, Mill, and Stable; held by Lease under the Executor of the late Mr. Rainford, for two fresh Lives (now in Being) and twenty-one Years.
Also four Dwelling Houses, fronting said Street, with a Cooperage, and a large Shade, being Land of Inheritance, and are now in the several Possessions of John Boichlin, Henry Rauthmell, James Laithwait, and Samuel Appleton; for further Particulars enquire of Henry Rauthmel or James Laithwait who will shew the Premises.

Advertisement for the sale of Gildart and Rauthmell's refinery.

the last decade of the eighteenth century, for when Waterworth died in 1800,[82] he was able to bequeath £2,000 to his friend William Tennant, who had been his assistant at the sugar house for several years. By 1815, the old refinery had passed to Unsworth and Holmes, but finally, by 1817, Unsworth had left the firm, and the following advertisement appeared in the *Liverpool Mercury* of Friday 31 January 1817: 'To be Let: Four Pan Sugar House situate in Rainford's garden in Liverpool, with a warehouse and counting house adjoining. The utensils may be taken at a valuation. For full particulars apply to Henry Holmes, jun. or Jas Holmes.'

Other Liverpool Refineries

The area between Matthew Street and Harrington Street had been the site of sugar refineries since the early eighteenth century. In fact, the refinery in John Street belonging to the Hughes' family, had been established longer than that of Rauthmell and Gildart, for in 1705, the town council had assessed Jonathan Hughes' sugar house and stock for rates at £1 4s 8d, and in 1708, that had been reduced to 12/-.[83] Unfortunately, that is all that is known of that refinery in those early years. However, there is an interesting reference to Jonathan in 1719 when Samuel Danvers of the Red Cross Street refinery bequeathed a gold ring to his friend Jonathan Hughes. Evidently, the early sugar refiners were closely connected socially, despite being rivals in trade. The next record of the Hughes' refinery is in the directory of 1766, and by then the business had passed to Richard Hughes.

The corner of Harrington Street and North John Street today. The site of John Knight's refinery.

Another refinery that was built near the corner of John Street and Harrington Street (Castle Hey), was that of John Knight & Co., and as we have seen, this was the place where the parish fire engine was kept in 1754 because it was a suitable place with easy access to two of the main thoroughfares of the town. Although these were two independent refineries in the 1760s, by 1774, they had been combined to form one refinery belonging to four partners – John Knight, who was also a merchant, John Hughes, presumably Richard Hughes' heir, Thomas Mears, and John Brownall.[84] As the industry expanded, more investment was needed, and so companies found it necessary to merge to increase their profit margins. This merger was a sign of things to come in the nineteenth century. John Knight died in 1774 and bequeathed his quarter of the business to his wife, but what exactly happened to the partnership after that is unclear. However, the refinery continued to operate, and in the directory of 1814-15,[85] the same site – No. 21 John Street – was listed as the refinery of Lorimer, Ellis & Company.[86]

All these refineries needed an endless supply of water. In fact, one manuscript dating from the eighteenth century specifically instructed sugar boilers to 'melt your sugar in a sufficient quantity of clean water'.[87] Any shortage could spell disaster for the refiners; as for instance, was recorded in the old minute book belonging to the Edinburgh Sugar House Company dated December 1765. It reads:

> 9 December 1765 – The boiler informs us that he was stopt in his boiling for want of water as there is a great scarcity in the town; recommend to Mr Hunter to solicit the magistrates to give an order to the man, who takes care of the water, to send down as much as will fill the lime cistern that the boiling be not stopt too long, as it will hurt the goods on the floor for the want of the proper heat to work them off.[88]

The magistrates in Edinburgh were very slow in responding, and boiling was stopped until 21 December, no doubt causing great hardship to the employees.

Any economy in the use of water resulted in the impurities remaining in the sugar. The finished product was a brownish colour, not the pure white demanded by the customers. In Liverpool, this demand for water could be met easily in the early days of refining, but as the refineries expanded and more were established in the town, some sugar boilers had problems with their water supply. Edmund Parker, the owner of a well and pump on Shaw's Brow (now William Brown Street), heard about the difficulties they were experiencing, and thought of a way that he could help – or profit – from them. He inserted an advertisement in the newspaper in November 1758 offering to supply water for sugar boiling from his pump at 9d per butt.[89]

Five years later, a new refinery had been built near this well to take advantage of the same water supply. This refinery was near the present entrance to the Kingsway Birkenhead tunnel, described as being 'on the west side of a certain street or place in Liverpool aforesaid called the Haymarket leading from the almshouses at the end of Dale Street to the east end of Lord Street and containing to the front of the Haymarket forty yards or thereabouts.'[90]

Again the partners, with one exception, were already established as merchants in Liverpool – Jonathan Blundell, Peter Holme, Ralph Earle, Thomas Hodgson, Patrick Black, and Thomas Lickbarrow. That exception was William Earle, also of Liverpool, who was described as an ironmonger. The partners each agreed to buy one seventh of the shares in the 'newly erected sugar house', and to work together for eleven years,

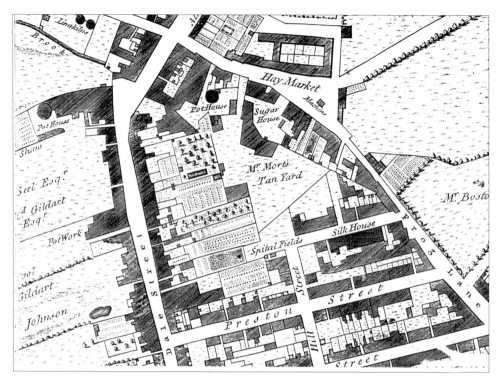

Perry's map of 1769 showing the sugar house of Jonathan Blundell and Company alongside the Haymarket. (*Reproduced by kind permission of Liverpool Record Office*)

The site of Blundell's refinery today. The tunnel entrance is on the site of the Haymarket.

with the option of extending that period. If any further capital was required by the business, it was to be supplied in the same proportion as the shares were held, and each partner was to bear an equal share of any losses. The business was to trade under the name of Jonathan Blundell & Company, and the partner Thomas Lickbarrow was appointed to be their accountant at a yearly salary of £100. In order that all the partners could monitor the progress of the business, the account book was to be kept in a 'convenient place in the sugar house freely available to all partners'. Several safeguards were put in place in order to guard the company's assets in the case of the death or bankruptcy of any of the partners. These measures proved very successful. Consequently, when Jonathan Blundell died in 1785 and the company was renamed T&W Earle, they were able to expand their interests in sugar, oil, iron, and silk by enlarging the partnership to include Thomas Molyneux.[91] However by the 1790s, the company had abandoned sugar refining altogether, and had concentrated on their more lucrative business as merchants, operating in both Fleet Street and Hanover Street.

Another of the refineries mentioned in the 1766 directory of Liverpool was that of George Campbell senior & Co of Duke Street. This was an area on the very edge of the town at that time; in fact a map of 1766 shows open fields within 100 yards of the sugar refinery. Nevertheless, it was not far from the old dock, so transporting the barrels of raw sugar to the refinery would not have been too difficult. The 1766 map shows the sugar refinery as being between Henry Street and Argyle Street, but evidently the complex expanded across Henry Street and fronted onto Duke Street, one of the main highways in Liverpool.[92] Again, the partners were also merchants trading with the West Indies, and in common with many of the other merchants, held property in the Indies. Indeed, when George Campbell died in 1769, he left property in the township of Everton in San Domingo. It is interesting that today in Everton, there is a St Domingo Road – possibly the site of the home of the Campbell family in the eighteenth century. One of the trustees of Campbell's will was another refiner Isaac Oldham, who as we have seen, was in partnership with Mr Caldwell in 1766, and owned the sugar house in Red Cross Street that was originally Danvers. A second trustee was Peter Orritt of Windle, who had also been in partnership with Isaac Oldham and who made sugar moulds for the refineries at his pottery. Thus, again we find

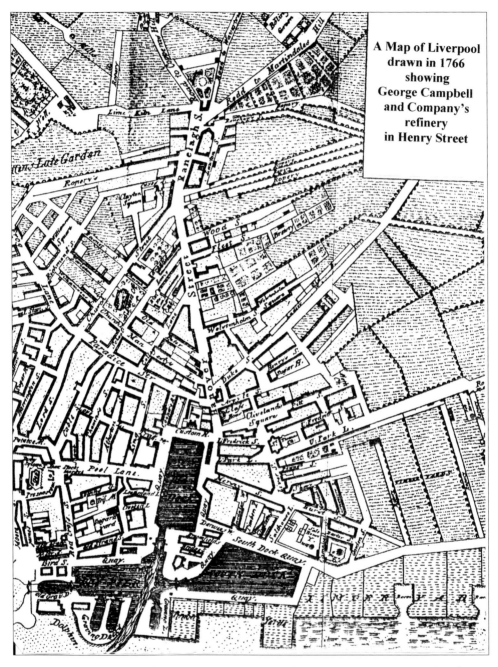

A map drawn in 1766 showing George Campbell's refinery in Henry Street. (*Reproduced by kind permission of Liverpool Record Office*)

Henry Street today. It is possible that these derelict warehouses were part of the Campbell refinery.

close social links as well as a commercial network operating among the sugar refiners and their suppliers.

Payments received for hogsheads of sugar are listed in the account books of this firm,[93] and one of these concerns money paid to Ralph Earle, a partner in the Jonathan Blundell refinery. Unfortunately, most of the entries are not sufficiently specific to attempt an analysis. However, one dated April 1769 lists 'proceeds of 149 hogsheads of sugar, £1,847 1s 0½d' from Samuel Horner of Dublin, thus giving us some idea of the value and extent of the trade at that time. A significant statistic was recorded by W. Enfield in 1773 when he wrote that about 6,000 hogsheads of sugar were annually refined in the sugar refineries of Liverpool.[94] If each hogshead sold for about £12, as the Campbell accounts suggest, the annual turnover of the town's sugar industry would have been approximately £72,000 – a huge amount when the value of money at that time is taken into account.

In 1770, some transactions were recorded with Fuhrer Wagner of Liverpool, but as there are no records of a refinery of that name in the town, nor of any partnership agreement including him, he was probably acting as an independent agent or broker at that time. The number of

Buck's Prospect of Liverpool showing Campbell's sugar house, the tall building behind the quayside properties at the right hand side of the etching. (*Reproduced by kind permission of Liverpool Record Office*)

Germans involved in the Liverpool sugar industry increased so much in the late eighteenth and early nineteenth centuries that by the 1870s there was a large colony – almost a German township – on the north-west boundary of the city.[95]

On Dale Street, opposite Hackins Hey and extending almost to Castle Street, was the last of the sugar house complexes named in the 1766 directory. It belonged to the Tarleton family, another group of merchants who had expanded into sugar refining. The family had been established in Liverpool for many years. In fact, on a map dated 1650, a plot of land stretching from the castle to the shore of the Mersey is called 'Tarleton's field'.[96] As we have seen, in the 1660s, Margaret Tarleton married the master of the *Hunter,* who brought what was probably the first cargo of sugar from the West Indies to Liverpool. In 1686, a member of the family Edward Tarleton, a ship's captain, was involved in transporting indentured servants to act as labourers for the tobacco growers in New England.[97] In fact, Nicholas Blundell recorded paying him £5 in 1704 for taking a tailor's son to Virginia to be apprentice to his brother Richard Blundell,[98] who was an agent for a merchant involved in the tobacco trade. However, when the trade in sugar began to prove more profitable, many of the Liverpool merchants – including the Tarleton family – lessened their commitments in New England, established new links with the West Indies, and also became involved in sugar refining in their home town.

In 1767, an unusual advertisement appeared in the *Liverpool Courier* on 31 December in which John Tarleton announced that he had a quantity of Granada sugar for sale to individual grocers. The refiners usually sold their sugar directly to the larger dealers, so it is unclear what prompted Tarleton to dispose of his sugar to smaller outlets. He actually mentioned in the advertisement that the sugar was 'very proper for the scale' – in other words not too sticky for them to weigh out for their customers. Also included in the sale were forty puncheons – small barrels – of Jamaican rum, probably the rest of the cargo from the Indies.[99]

The Tarleton family continued to expand their interests, until by 1773 they had considerable estates in the Indies. In fact in his will of that date, John Tarleton lists:

> My estate in the Island of Carriacou, America, being about 500 and 9 acres of land with the buildings I have erected there, the Negroes and all other stock I have thereon … my house or store in the town of Grand Ance on the said island … my house and store in the town of St George in the island of Grenada … [and the] Bulfield Estate in Dominica bought for me by John Finch for £4,320 Stirling.

Much of this property would have been vast sugar fields providing the raw materials for the Tarleton refinery in Liverpool. It is significant that Tarleton still regarded the Negroes as part of his stock, not his employees, when the anti-slavery debate was already beginning to gain momentum.

When he died in 1773, John Tarleton also owned a large piece of land extending from Castle Street to John Street, between Dale Street and Cook Street. On Castle Street, one of Liverpool's main thoroughfares, he had built three large houses; two were leased to Mr Patten and Mr Stanford, and the third was empty. Behind these was the sugar house complex, consisting of a large sugar refinery, two warehouses, a dwelling house for the sugar boiler, a stable, a warehouse, a counting house, and other buildings. The counting house was leased to Mr Wetherhead, possibly the firm's accountant. It is interesting that there was neither a hen house, a swine yard, nor a summer house as there had been in

Castle Street in the eighteenth century. (*Reproduced from a painting by W. G. Herdman, courtesy of the Athenaeum Club*)

Samuel Danvers' sugar house complex in 1719. Liverpool had lost many of its rural aspects and had become an urban settlement by the 1770s.

As we have seen, many of the workers in the refineries lived either in the sugar house or in houses nearby. The long tradition whereby apprentices lived in the house of their master had developed into the custom that all the unmarried labourers lived at their workplace. Of course, it was essential that the sugar boiler was always available whenever production was in process. Therefore, it was necessary for him to live either within the factory environs – as he did in the Tarleton's complex – or in very close proximity to it. The other workers usually lived in or near to the refinery because they were employed in shifts in order that the refinery could be constantly in operation. If the vats were allowed to cool, the sugar set and caused endless problems. In the Edinburgh sugar house, the boiler, the 'upstairsman', and the cooper all lived in the sugar house or in rooms attached to it.[100] In fact, one pensioner from MacFie's sugar refiners recorded that, until as late as 1880, unmarried workers slept in the sugar house in Liverpool.

Originally, John Tarleton had several partners, but by the 1770s, only John Backhouse – another merchant – survived. However a short time

Sweeting Street off Castle Street
the site of the Tarleton refinery
complex. The four-storey building
was probably the actual refinery.
(*Reproduced from a painting by
W. G. Herdman, courtesy of the
Athenaeum Club*)

before he died, Tarleton bought Backhouse's three eighths shareholding, thus dissolving the partnership and taking over the premises. That enabled him to lease the whole complex to a completely new sugar house partnership for £175 per annum.[101] Although he did not mention the name of the new partnership in his will, it was probably headed by William Skelhorne, for as we have seen earlier, by the 1790s and until the turn of the century, the directories record that William Skelhorne & Co. had a refinery behind No. 12 Castle Street, the site of the Tarleton refinery. In the meantime, the Tarleton family had abandoned their interest in refining and concentrated on their roles as merchants in the town.

Despite all the hard work involved in developing the industry, several of the sugar refiners and their families were also concerned in various philanthropic ventures. For instance, Stephen Waterworth, William Gregson, and James Okill were trustees of the Blue Coat Hospital, while Thomas Beckwith acted as auditor for the Dispensary.[102] Nevertheless, they still found time for enjoyment according to Samuel Derrick, the Master of Ceremonies at Bath.[103] When he visited Liverpool, he was very interested in the social life of the town, and recorded his impressions of

Castle Street today.

the leisure activities of many prominent people. He mentioned that two
of the leading sugar bakers were members of 'Ye Ugly Face Clubb',[104]
founded in 1743 and closed 1754. The club, which banned gambling,
met once a fortnight at the Exchange Coffee House in Water Street, and
dined once a quarter in various other eating houses. Evidently, the sugar
bakers did not spend all their time amassing huge fortunes, but of course,
many of their lucrative deals would have been made at their clubs.

By 1815, when another reliable list of sugar bakers was published,
none of the firms that were recorded in the eighteenth century remained.
Surprisingly, as late as 1882, there were still only eight sugar refineries in
Liverpool,[105] the same number as there had been in 1766. In fact, both
Liverpool and London had eight refineries at that time. The nineteenth
century saw many sugar refiners, who were well established in other
towns, move to Liverpool either to set up new businesses or possibly to
take over the old established ones under new names. The MacFie family,
who started refining in Greenock in 1788, came to Liverpool in 1838,
the Fairrie family who had opened their refinery – also in Greenock
– in 1797, moved to Liverpool in 1847, and in 1859, Henry Tate, who
was then a grocer, became a partner of John Wright, a sugar refiner
in Manesty Lane. The history of most of these later sugar refiners has
already been researched and recorded in several publications.

It would have been interesting to be able to quantify the increase in
sugar refining in Liverpool during the years between Alleyn Smith's first

refinery in the 1660s and the end of the eighteenth century, but although details of the ownership of the refineries remain, there are no meaningful records of their output. However, one statistic that gives some idea of the success of the industry is the amount of sugar imported into Liverpool. It rose dramatically during the eighteenth century, from 760 tons in 1704 to 46,000 tons in 1810.[106] Of course, not all that sugar was refined in Liverpool, for some would have been distributed to refineries in Chester and Warrington. Nevertheless, the quantities involved are very impressive. Although statistics for industrial growth in Liverpool for the eighteenth century are non-existent, the information that is available does provide an interesting picture of the growth of the sugar industry, and incidentally also charts the parallel urbanisation of the town.

CHAPTER 3

The Chester Refineries

The sugar refining industry in Chester had a very different history from that in Liverpool. It was not sited in a good position for an industry that relied on imports from the Indies, and unfortunately, it was subjected to a series of tragedies that had disastrous results for the refineries.

The earliest recorded sugar refiner in Chester was Anthony Henthorne, who settled in the Whitefriars district in April 1669. It is possible that, like Alleyn Smith of Liverpool, he had moved north from London following the great plague and fire. Certainly his close friend, Giles Vanburgh, father of the famous architect Sir John Vanburgh, moved his family north in 1667 as a result of those tragedies. Although it has been suggested that this close friendship was the result of their joint involvement in sugar refining,[107] there is no definite evidence to prove that this was the case. However, the Vanburgh family had been merchants in Antwerp and Haarlem before they moved to London to escape religious persecution. Consequently, as Dutch merchants trading in sugar with the Dutch South American colonies, the family would have been well acquainted with their customers, the London sugar refiners, among whom was Anthony Henthorne. Thus, it is very likely that as a result of this connection, the two families became friendly and moved north together.

The Henthorne family settled in Chester in property that had been acquired at the dissolution of the monasteries by the Egerton family. In 1651, that property had been leased by Richard Harrison, a beer brewer, and seemingly he had built a brewery on the east side of Weavers Lane

The house where the Vanburgh and later the Henthorne families are thought to have lived.

between Common Hall Lane and Whitefriars Lane. It was in the early 1670s that this Richard Harrison leased a dwelling house in St Bridget's parish to Giles Vanburgh, who later passed the house on to his friend Anthony Henthorne.[108] It was a substantial house, for in 1673, it was taxed for seven hearths.

Soon afterwards, Henthorne leased the rest of the brewery buildings from Harrison and began to convert them into his sugar refinery, which was completed by 1677. Finally, in 1679, Henthorne bought Harrison's interest in the whole complex. Confusingly, the site fell under the jurisdiction of three different parishes – Holy Trinity in the North, St Martins in the south, and St Bridgets to the east at the corner of Whitefriars Lane and Bridge Street. Consequently, Henthorne's tax assessments were also divided between the three parishes; for example, in 1680, he paid tax on his house, sugar house, and garden to St Bridgets, and in 1685, he was assessed for the 'Fryary' in St Martins, and he paid the poor rate at Holy Trinity.[109]

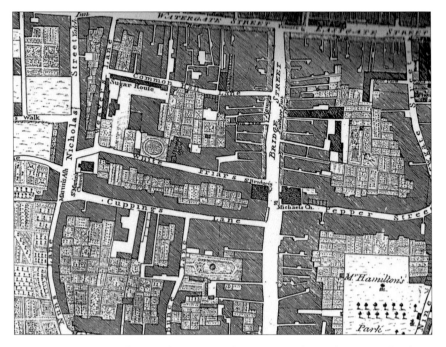

James Hunter's map of 1789 showing Henthorne's sugar house between Whitefriars and Common Hall Lane. (*Reproduced by kind permission of the Chester History and Heritage Centre*)

We know very little about those who worked at this sugar refinery in the seventeenth century. They are the unrecorded majority. However, John Woosey, one of Henthorne's labourers from 1677 until 1678, appeared in a case at the Lancaster Assizes, and among the deposition documents is a description of how he moved about the area, seeking employment in various sugar refineries. At first he was apprenticed at Danver's refinery in Liverpool, then he moved to Ormskirk and was involved in the foundation of a refinery in that town.[110] When that failed, he moved to work for Henthorne in Chester for a couple of years, before being imprisoned for debt at Lancaster Castle. This case demonstrates that there was some mobility among the sugar boiling workforce, and also that there were means of communication between the workers in the various refineries in the North West.

By 1678, his employer Anthony Henthorne was recognised as one of the leading business men in Chester and was allowed to purchase the freedom of the city. The fact that his freedom was not hereditary, and that he had to prove his worth before the assembly would grant him the privilege, suggests that the family had indeed moved into the city, possibly in the late 1660s. His freedom cost him £50, together with a payment to the leave lookers of the same amount, which he had paid in tolls to them in the previous year.[111] Three years later, Anthony Henthorne was involved in a dispute concerning the payment of duties on a quantity of sugar that he had imported through the port of Chester. Whether he thought that as a freeman he should be exempt from such duties, or whether he objected to the amount that he was charged, is unclear. Nevertheless, although he was summoned to appear before the Mayor, justices of the peace, and the Recorder, he stubbornly refused to settle the account.[112] Consequently, the officers confiscated a large quantity of his sugar and stored it in the Common Hall. The case dragged on, and in 1683, the assembly ordered that the case should be heard in the city's court.[113] Henthorne remained adamant, and instead of paying up, he gathered support from other merchants who also objected to paying the large import duties. The assembly was not impressed by the ever-increasing support that Henthorne rallied around his cause,

Etching of the Common Hall. (*Reproduced by kind permission of the principal archivist for Cheshire Record Office Ref: VPR 3/CHES/47*)

and in 1685, they published an order defending their officers and the traditional customs of the city.[114]

The following year, the case came before the aldermen of the city, including Thomas Simpson, William Ince, William Wilne, Francis Skellern, and William Allen, all of whom agreed that the matter should go to arbitration. They decreed that, 'If Mr Henthorne refused to abide by their determination, the murringers were to sell the sugar and pay the duty out of the proceeds, paying the surplus to Henthorne.' The murringers, or murengers – the officials originally appointed to keep the city walls in repair – were by this time responsible for the city's finances. The assembly was so exasperated by Henthorne's stubbornness that they decreed that the matter had to be settled by 25 July of that year.[115]

By 19 July, the referees had come to a decision. In the end, they seemed to have been swayed by the support given to Henthorne, for although he owed the city authorities £51 11s 6d in custom dues, they decided that they would reduce the amount to £20. This was described as an acknowledgement of the trade he had brought to the city. Henthorne paid the required amount to the murringers and the confiscated sugar was returned to him. That was not the end of the matter, for he still had to pay the keeper of the common hall 13s for storing the sugar. However, at least the expenses of the leave lookers for the 'seizure of the goods and their carriage to the hall' were to be paid out of the £20 that Henthorne had paid in custom dues.

From this case, it is clear that Henthorne was not afraid to challenge those in authority in defence of what he believed to be right. He showed the same attitude in regard to his religious faith. After the passing of the 1662 Act of Uniformity and the ejection of many clergymen from the Anglican Church, their supporters met for services in private houses. Henthorne was one of the leading dissenters in Chester, and he invited William Cooke, a minister ejected from St Michaels in Chester, to hold meetings in his house. They were very successful and so when the congregation increased, Henthorne offered them a large outbuilding near the friary to use as a chapel. Not content to cater only for the local clergy, he invited the famous dissenting minister Matthew Henry to Chester to preach in this new friary chapel.[116]

Like Daniel Danvers and Richard Cleveland in Liverpool, he disobeyed the rule of the established Church that all Christians should attend their

Matthew Henry's Chapel which was built on Henthorne's land and was supported by the family. (*Reproduced by kind permission of Chester History and Heritage Centre*)

parish church on a Sunday. The Church authorities could not allow a leading citizen to defy their rules, especially when he was the employer of a large labour force. They ordered Henthorne to appear before the Consistory Court in Chester in 1682, and witnesses were called to testify that he had not worshipped at his parish church for some time. One of these said that he had seen Henthorne in church only twice in five years, and even then he had entered the building in the middle of the service. Another deponent described seeing Henthorne in church behaving very irreverently 'with his hat hanging on one side of his head all the while', and although he had 'observed him pretty well because it was an unusual posture ... he did not see him take it off or move it to any other posture'.[117] The result of this trial has been lost, but the only punishment that could be imposed on Henthorne would have been a fine and the moral disgrace of being brought before the court to answer charges.

Despite these encounters with the customs officials and the clergy, the Henthorne family continued to be respected in the city. Anthony's son Samuel, who owned half of 'The Friary' at the time of his marriage in 1686, was made a freeman on 28 July 1686,[118] and two years later, his brother John received the same honour. When their father died,

The site of Henthorne's refinery today. This derelict warehouse probably originated as Henthorne's refinery.

Samuel inherited the sugar refinery, but unfortunately, he died shortly afterwards. Samuel was an extremely rich man, and left about £1,000 in his will dated 1695.[119] In it, he bequeathed £400 each to his son William and to his daughter Elizabeth when they reached the age of twenty-one, while his wife was to receive £200. It is significant that Matthew Henry, the dissenting minister, witnessed the will, for it confirms that the Henthorne family continued to support the dissenters until the closing years of the seventeenth century. As we have seen, this relationship between the early sugar refiners of Chester and the dissenters of that city had parallels in similar relationships between the Danvers family and the early dissenters of Liverpool.[120] This could indicate a possible link between the two families.

Exactly what happened to the sugar refinery on the death of Samuel is problematical. However, a sugar baker Ralph Wynne lived in the parish of St Bridget in 1718,[121] and another sugar boiler Joseph Blease, who belonged to St Martin's parish, was buried at Holy Trinity church in 1723.

Right: The East Gate, Chester at the time when the Hincks family lived there.

Below: Eastgate today.

The fact that these two skilled sugar boilers lived in the district where
the Henthorne refinery was situated suggests that they were employed
there, and that the sugar house had continued to operate under a new
partnership. The fact that John Marsden, described as a sugar baker, was
a creditor and administrator of the will of Joseph Blease, could indicate
that it was he who employed the two boilers, or possibly that he was in
partnership with them. Certainly the Marsden family, at first John and
later Thomas, were closely concerned with sugar refining in the area for
many years, as we shall see. The exact location of their workplace is
unclear, but it seems possible that John Marsden and his partners had
taken over the Henthorne sugar refinery when the family sold it.

The Hincks family, who lived in Eastgate Street and owned several
other properties, were the next sugar refiners to be recorded in Chester.[122]
However, it was not until 1757 that John Hincks actually became a
partner in a new sugar refinery. Plans had been made to erect another
sugar house on 'that parcel of land ... used as a coal yard and rope walk
lying to the south side of Cuppings Lane in the parish of St Martins' in
the early 1750s.[123] Nothing was done until Thomas Adams, realising the
potential of the site, leased it from Thomas Prescott on 20 July 1752,
with the intention of building a sugar house. He told Prescott his plans,
and the landlord insisted on inserting a clause in the lease, stipulating
that if he did erect a refinery on the land within three years, Adams
would pay him an extra £50.[124] This seems a strange arrangement,
but evidently, Prescott realised that his holding would be much more
valuable if the building took place, and so he insisted on being paid some
compensation. In fact, Adams lost interest and abandoned the project
during the following year, leaving Prescott with the undeveloped land
again available for lease.

The following year, another tenant was found, namely Benjamin
Wilson, a sugar baker from Liverpool, who agreed that, if he built
the sugar house, he would pay Prescott £50 within one month of its
completion.[125] Although it was Wilson who leased the land, he had
wealthy associates, including the Hincks family, who also realised the
potential of the proposed refinery and so agreed to become shareholders
if a company was formed. It was decided that £16,000 would be required
to cover the costs of the building and the equipment, and also to provide
a working capital for buying the raw sugar, hiring the labourers, and

so on. Even though this seemed an immense amount of money at the time, the partners were convinced of the viability of the project and agreed to provide the capital. Consequently, the partnership agreement was drawn up on 21 March 1757. Joseph Manesty, a merchant based in Liverpool, provided half of the capital and took half the shares, while John Hincks and Benjamin Wilson each had a quarter of the shares as their investment. Wilson agreed to pay the fine that would be levied by the Porte Mote Court once the complex consisting of a dwelling house, sugar house, warehouse, and stable was completed.[126]

Two other documents, dated a couple of days before the partnership agreement, appear to record an early form of mortgage.[127] They involved John Parr, a merchant, and Edward Parr, an apothecary, who leased the complex from the partnership for one year for the payment of 5s. I think the partners had borrowed money from the Parrs, and as part of the deal, the partners had leased their premises to the Parrs for an extremely small amount as a form of surety. The involvement of the Parr family suggests some link with the family of the same name from Warrington, who were also merchants, and were concerned later in refining.[128] More significantly and later still, the Parr family moved into banking. These connections between the Warrington refiners and the Chester partnership, including merchants from Liverpool, again indicate a close economic relationship between the various refiners in the south of the area.

As Benjamin Wilson was an experienced sugar baker, it was agreed that he should act as manager for a salary of £80 a year. Meanwhile Manesty, who had experience of the market in Liverpool, was to act as their agent, and when suitable cargoes arrived in the port, he would buy unrefined sugar in quantity for the refinery. A letter sent by Manesty to his partners in Chester on 28 February 1758 gives a typical example of his financial dealings.[129] He acknowledged the receipt of £698 4s in bills of exchange and copper (coins), which he was to hold in credit for the sugar house. Presumably that was to be his working capital. He then described the current state of the market that had been influenced by the unexpected arrival of two ships from Jamaica carrying sugar from Barbados. Although the ships were still being unloaded, already about half of the sugar had been sold and was destined for the Dublin market. The merchants had paid between 39s and 43s per hogshead for the unrefined sugar. Manesty had bid 39s each for 50 hogsheads of what he described as 'heavy Barbados' sugar – the kind he knew Wilson would prefer. However at at the time of writing, he did not know whether his bid had been accepted. To assure his colleagues that he was not paying too much for the sugar, he told them that during the previous week, Mr Patten of the Warrington refinery had paid 40s for a quantity of what he described as 'ordinary Jamaicas', presumably an inferior type of sugar.

If Manesty's bid was successful, he arranged to 'ship them next spring tides', in other words, he would send the hogsheads of sugar from Liverpool to Chester by sea. Transport by sea was the only real option for fifty huge barrels of sugar at that time, as horse drawn wagons could not carry such weighty loads along the muddy tracks, which were the only roads in the area at that time. The port books of Liverpool record many examples of ships transporting goods into the port of Liverpool from Chester. There is an interesting entry dating from December 1660, when the ferry boat the *Eastham* carried a mixed cargo including redwood, oil, soap, indigo, and 0.75 cwt of molasses, 0.25 cwt of loaf sugar, and 30 lb of brown candy between the two centres.[130] Such a cargo poses the question of where that sugar had been refined. The fact that the boat was described as a ferryboat suggests that it was used only on the short trip from Chester to Liverpool, even though the cargo had originated in the West Indies. Had it been brought from the Indies to London to be refined, and then continued around the coast, being off-loaded at various ports including Chester, as was the usual practice in Tudor and early Stuart times? However, there is the interesting possibility that the loaf sugar had been refined in Chester and had been loaded onto the ferry boat to continue its voyage to Liverpool for sale or distribution. That would mean that a sugar boiler was at work in Chester before the days of Henthorne's refinery, but unfortunately, that cannot be proved without more evidence.

Manesty's letter suggests that transport by sea from Liverpool to Chester was proving difficult at that time. He reports that he will have to wait for the spring tides, so evidently a high tide was necessary to enable the heavily laden boats to reach the port of Chester. The River Dee was gradually silting up and becoming too shallow for them. This was very ominous for the future of Chester's refineries. Any delay in the delivery of the raw sugar could mean that their competitors in Liverpool had the advantage of being able to sell their sugar long before the Chester refiners could meet the demand.

Manesty continued to report to his partners all that had been happening in Liverpool. There was a slightly envious note when he reported that Mr 'Rothmell' (Rauthmell) had started his new partnership at a very fortunate time, as we have seen, for he had benefited from cheaper raw sugar. The markets for both refined and raw sugar were never stable. In fact, it was said by a dealer in 1745, 'Nothing can be more fluctuating than the market for sugar, the continuance of an easterly wind for a few weeks shall raise it, and a westerly wind with the bare expectation of the arrival of ships shall lower it again.'[131]

Evidently, Benjamin Wilson had asked what prices the other refiners were charging for their molasses – the impure sugar left after the sugar had been partially refined. Molasses was sold to distillers to be used in the production of rum, and it was important to the new refinery to know exactly what their competitors were charging. Manesty reported that in recent days, molasses had been sold at 24s, 25s, and 26s.[132] He also informed his colleagues that the London merchants had ordered a quantity for the next six months at 24s per hogshead, and that the Lancaster Sugar House and Mr Marsden, possibly the administrator of John Blease's will, had agreed to sell them all they had.

It is significant that Manesty advised Wilson not to sell his stocks in a hurry, because he believed that if these orders from London were fulfilled, there would be a shortage of molasses. Then Wilson would be able to command a much higher price for his produce. In fact, Manesty assured his partner that Mr Tarleton, another Liverpool refiner, was determined not sell his molasses under 30s. He had received a letter from a Mr Bradshaw of London, which had confirmed that the price in some parts of London was already 30s, and Mr Bradshaw was confident that the prices in the capital would rise in the near future. After he had ended his letter, Manesty received news that appeared to confirm that this forecast was correct, so he added after his signature, 'All the Jamaica fleet for London and Bristol are lost or taken but one.' They were victims of the French fleet in the Seven Years War (1756-1763). It seemed certain that when only one ship remained to deliver raw sugar to the south of

England, the price of molasses processed in the North and destined for the London market would rise.

In the same letter, Manesty made a comment that must have worried his partners. He admitted that he was having great difficulty trying to get prompt payment from his clients, particularly from a customer called Barker. Consequently, to avoid any further trouble he destroyed the order that Barker had already placed for a further supply of sugar. Manesty advised Wilson to 'draw' on Barker for the amount he owed, in other words to obtain goods to the amount owed from Barker's company until the debt was cleared. Despite this disconcerting news, Wilson was reluctant to lose Barker's custom, and told Manesty not to be too hasty. In the next letter written a week later, the agent agreed reluctantly to call on Barker, but declared that he did not expect that Barker would have changed his attitude and be willing to pay off his debt to the refinery.[133]

In his letter, Wilson also replied that he doubted his agent's prediction regarding the rise in prices. As he explained, some of his contacts had told him that sugar bakers were short of orders and prices were dropping. Manesty was obviously irritated by Wilson's doubts, and replied, 'Your friends who advise that sugar bakers press for orders, must be green. They will write and tell a thousand falsehoods to my knowledge to get a shilling.'[134] Consequently, full of confidence in his predictions, Manesty bought fifty-five hogsheads of Jamaican sugar at 40s each, and at the time of writing (5 March), he had already shipped the sugar to Chester on the *Barns* and the *Chester*, two boats that could negotiate the shallow waters of the River Dee. Of course, that would be at the time of the spring tides, so it was very important to take advantage of the deeper water. To dispel Wilson's doubts still further, Manesty reported that Mr Marsden, who had sold to the London merchants at 24s, had no more left in his warehouse, and could only sell to customers who were willing to wait three months for delivery. Marsden, he said, was confident that a shortage was developing in London, and declared that he would not sell locally for 24s per hogshead, but in future would send his supplies to London where, presumably, they would command a higher price. As Manesty waited for the expected demand to come from London with the attendant price rises, he advised Wilson to stock up supplies in readiness, and if he was short of space, to send twenty or thirty hogsheads of molasses back to Liverpool for storage. Indeed his optimism knew no bounds, and he remarked that he expected prices to rise to 80s before May Day. He assured his partners that there were no stocks in the warehouses, and as soon as the molasses were produced, they were sold.[135]

Fifteen days later, disaster struck. Manesty wrote, 'It is a great grief to me that this matter has so happened, but as I could not raise cash to pay the excise of rum and some other demands pressing, I had no remedy left but to shut my doors.' All the optimism had led him to invest too heavily in supplies of sugar and he had no money left to meet the payments that were due on behalf of his other businesses. Evidently, he was also a distiller in his own right, and so had to pay the taxes levied on rum. This tragic misjudgement was to have a dire effect on the newly established sugar refining company, and personally on his partners in Chester. Manesty assured Wilson that he had used bills of exchange in his own name when he paid for most of the sugar that he had bought on behalf of the Chester Sugar House, and so the company would not be liable. According to him, there was only one of their parcels of raw sugar for which payment was outstanding, and that was owed to a Mr James. Seemingly, Wilson had thought Mr James had overcharged them, and so Manesty had delayed paying him. Otherwise, no-one else had any claim on the Chester Sugar House.

Then Manesty continued to list other transactions in which he had been involved. He included many other refiners from the area among his clients, including both Mr Patten of the Warrington refinery and Mr Wakefield of the Red Cross Street refinery in Liverpool, both of whom had bought supplies of sugar, imported by Messrs Rigby. Mr Okill, another Liverpool refiner and later a partner of Mr Wakefield, was also involved with both the agent and the Chester Sugar House. Seemingly, Manesty had bought a quantity of sugar from Mr Okill for the Chester partnership. However, as the hogsheads were waiting for transport and had not been moved from the warehouse, Manesty was confident that Okill would accept the sugar back again for resale and not press for payment. Yet again, he had misjudged the situation.

On 15 April, the distraught Wilson received a letter from Okill's solicitor William Pickance of Liverpool, demanding payment and expressing surprise that Wilson had not expected to be liable for the sugar that had been bought for his company. Pickance claimed that the sugar had been delivered to the agent and was not, as Manesty claimed, still in Okill's warehouse. The solicitor had also been contacted by Mr James to press Wilson for payment. Consequently, on behalf of his two clients, Pickance threatened to 'take such methods as the law demands' if Wilson did not pay all he owed immediately.[136] This seems very harsh when it was only a month since Wilson first received the news of Manesty's difficulties. The solicitor threatened that he would 'take measures accordingly' unless Wilson replied by return of post. If no reply was received, 'Silence shall take for a refusal of payment.'

Wilson was already under great financial pressure from Manesty, who claimed, falsely it would seem, that the Chester company owed him for two parcels of fine sugar valued at £110 and £240. That cannot have been the case, for Manesty had already admitted that he had been forced to 'pass' Wilson's notes – bills of exchange that Manesty was holding for the company as part of his working capital – but he would repay them by the sale of goods in hand. One for £500 had been paid to the bank and another had been paid to Messrs Harts in Warrington.

Finally, Manesty turned in his letter to the practical details concerning the actual refining of sugar at Chester. There were seven hogsheads of sugar being refined for a Mr Griffiths, and Manesty advised Wilson to go ahead and charge for the sugar as he judged correct, considering that they had been bought for £20 6s 7d. Then he added a reluctant note:

> I suppose you'll boil all up & make an end so far as relates me and call in other partners instead.

> I am very much sir, your humble servant,
> Jo Manesty.[137]

After much deliberation, the remaining partners decided that they would continue in business, despite all the trauma of Manesty's bankruptcy. Both John Hincks and Benjamin Wilson were completely bewildered as to how to proceed. The most important thing was to deal with the legal aspect of the affair, and so they asked the solicitors Lowe, Widderes, and Cross to advise them. They dealt with the creditor's pressing demands, and then nothing could be done until December 1764 when the Chancery

The site of the Hincks' refinery today.

Court declared Manesty bankrupt.[138] The creditors agreed that the sugar house in Chester could not be involved in the ongoing negotiations regarding Manesty's estate. Consequently, the lawyers were free at last to negotiate with Manesty and his assignees to convey his part of the sugar house to Wilson and Hincks.[139] First of all, the partnership had to be redrafted, and in 1764 a new partnership agreement for twenty-one years was drawn up.[140] Manesty's share in the sugar house was conveyed legally by his assignees to Wilson and Hincks, who then could continue in business with their affairs in order.

However, that was not to be. All the worry had affected Wilson's health, and in 1767 he died, leaving a very detailed will including explicit instructions as to what was to be done with regard to the sugar house. Realising that he was the only partner who had a real working knowledge of the trade, he instructed his executors to have all the new sugar 'speedily worked up', and to sell all the refined sugar from the moulds. Then his share in the premises, the utensils, and any sugar that remained was to be valued and sold. He gave instructions that John Hincks, his partner, whom he described significantly as a 'banker', was to be given the first chance to buy the goods that were offered for sale, but it was important that Wilson's investment in the business was realised for the sake of his heirs.

Although there are no documents explaining exactly how the executors realised Wilson's share of the business, the sugar house was still in operation several years later under the control of the Hincks family. Therefore it would seem that, despite not being a skilled sugar baker, John Hincks had bought Wilson's share of the company and so had enabled it to continue trading. Unfortunately, four years later John Hincks died. He named his wife Arabella and his brother Robert Hincks as executors of his will, but left no precise instructions about the future of the sugar house, which meant that yet again, new agreements had to be drawn up by the lawyers.

In 1770, a detailed audit had been made of the sugar that was in the process of refining, showing that it amounted in value to about £5,000.[141] Nevertheless Robert, the executor, was not satisfied that the refinery was making any real profit. In fact, he made a statement in which he declared that the capital for the sugar house had been raised from various bonds and securities, and although he had stood surety for some of those, he had never been repaid. He also asserted that, although his brother John had promised him a fourth share of the profits made by the refinery in recognition of the care and assistance that he had given him, he had not received any payment whatsoever. Understandably, he did not want anything more to do with the business. However, John's widow Arabella was adamant that she wanted the business to pass to her young son Thomas Cowper Hincks. Consequently, despite Robert's serious misgivings about the prospect of continuing the business, he finally agreed to sell the sugar house to Arabella for 10s.[142]

While the family decided on its future, the refinery continued to operate on a much reduced scale. They approached Sam Norcot, an experienced sugar baker of Water Street in Manchester, for his advice on continuing the business, and at his request the accounts for 'Mrs Hincks' Sugar House' were compiled. Those for the year 1775-1776 provided sound evidence that the sugar house was in real difficulty. They listed the stock of sugars remaining in the house as being worth £6,096 19s. During that year, raw sugar worth £9,427 7s 2d had been bought by the company. The workmen's wages totalled £145 1s, while salaries cost the company £181 10s. Altogether, the audit valued the company's assets at over £14,071, but that included book debts of over £5,854, rising to £7,581 by 1776. Although it is very difficult at this distance to understand these accounts, a loss of over £364 in the year was definitely recorded.[143] After studying the accounts, visiting the refinery, and making enquiries about the viability of continuing the business from various merchants and businessmen in the district, Norcot wrote to the family in April 1777. His verdict was that it would be very unwise of Mrs Hincks to continue her plan of 'beginning a sugar house'.[144] In fact, one of his contacts in Liverpool had replied, 'There's not the least prospect of beginning a sugar house with success in all this year and consequently not of upwards of twelve months.' Finally, Norcot concluded that he 'would not encourage Mrs Hincks unless [he] saw a very clear prospect of success, which at present [he] did not'.

He gave the widow an alternative plan of how it would be wise to proceed. The hogsheads of bastard sugar should be melted and processed, and the remaining syrup should be boiled up 'to make powder loaves'. The top of the lime cistern should be mended, as well as 'all little repairs the house may want'. 'The horse might be sent to work for his keep', and most of the remaining equipment that was deteriorating rapidly should be sold. He thought that coopers would 'give good prices' for the old casks, staves, and headings that he had noticed lying about in the refinery, for indeed such things would only fall to pieces and rot away if they were left. As the refinery had far more coal than was required, some of that could be sold. The incidental materials – the blue paper and the twine – used in the everyday processes in the refinery could be sold to Mr Hesketh, who would give a fair price for them. No doubt this Mr Hesketh would be the sugar refiner who had a sugar house in Warrington. There the industry was proving increasingly profitable as improvements to the waterways brought easier access to both the raw materials and to the swelling population of Manchester and the surrounding cotton towns.

Sam Norcot warned Mrs Hincks that the workers' wages were adding unnecessarily to the mounting costs. He recommended that she should instruct the sugar boiler, who was responsible for hiring and firing the labourers involved in processing the sugar, to dismiss his workers. He suggested that the workers should be given the promise that if the refinery ever resumed full production and workers were needed again, they would be the first to be considered and would be paid a bonus for returning promptly to the sugar house. However, he advised her not to mention an exact sum in case it was 'more than they are worth ... if the house stands long'. In fact, he also warned her that if the refinery did reopen and it was necessary to pay wages lower than the workers had been led to expect, 'that might bring on a train of bad consequences'.

Then, he turned his attention to the wages of the clerk and the boiler. He felt that there was really insufficient work for the two of them, and so he suggested that their wages should be reduced after they had been given three month's notice. He explained that such an economy would only be possible if there had been no legal agreement concerning their wages. Norcot must have been a very shrewd man for he continued, 'Your best way would be to weigh up all the sugar in the house immediately before you tell 'em your mind, and keep that list of the weight and quantities – and make a memorandum in the day book that the sales after that may tally with your account of stocks.' He realised that once the employees knew that they were likely to lose their jobs, they would be tempted to help themselves to some of the stock.

Evidently, Benjamin Wilson's heir had continued to sell sugar from the refinery, and when Norcot visited, he had noticed that the prices Wilson had been charging were too low. He remarked that the price could safely be increased by £2, and he was sure that the price of candy could similarly be increased to £88 or £90. Again, it is difficult to determine exactly what quantities of sugar or candy (partially refined sugar) were involved, but the message was clear, and he also urged Wilson to 'strive to sell the goods', as 'sugar don't go better by keeping too long, but worse'. Then, Norcot gave the family yet another piece of advice concerning the insurance of the premises. If the sugar house did not 'communicate' with the warehouse, the insurance could be reduced. The risk of fire was very great, and if the premises were separated, that risk would be reduced and so would the premium. Norcot ended his letter by promising that if the family felt they needed any help in the future, he would be happy to advise them.

It would seem that they definitely needed more help, for by August 1777, the total debts amounted to £4,918 11d, and of those, £1,119 16s 1d were listed as bad debts that were unlikely to be paid.[145] Nevertheless, despite all Mr Norcot's warnings, the stubborn Arabella decided to carry on the business. She found a new partner Mr. Boult, described as a 'grocer' who had been involved in delivering sugar to various customers. Possibly that meant that he was a middleman, a wholesaler, buying in quantity from the refineries, re-packing the sugar in smaller quantities, and then selling it on to ordinary shopkeepers. By August 1777, proposals had been drawn up for yet another new partnership agreement, this time between Arabella, acting on behalf of her son, and Mr Boult.[146] The partnership was to last for twenty-one years, but could be terminated after fourteen years by either party if they gave twelve month's notice. The new business – still in Cuppings Lane – was to be conducted under the name of Hincks and Boult, and each of the partners agreed to invest £5,000 in the project. All the utensils that remained in the sugar house were to count as part of Arabella's investment, and she was also to be credited with the money arising from the outstanding debts that were – hopefully – going to be collected 'with all convenient speed'. The house, garden, and warehouse were to be leased to 'the concern', presumably by Arabella, at a rent to be determined 'by one or more independent people conversant in the b usiness'.

Although the partnership was not legally to come into force until the following Christmas, it was decided that a quantity of raw sugar should be bought and that refining should begin immediately. Mr Boult was to be paid £100 a year 'for his extra trouble in the conduct of the business', and if the business prospered and he needed to employ a clerk to help him, that sum was to be increased to £146. The unusual partnership agreement contains several clauses that give an insight into the characters of the people involved. For instance if Mr Boult, who evidently enjoyed the social side of the business, found that he was under considerable expense in 'treating customers', he was to receive an additional allowance, but that was not to exceed £20 a year. Another unusual clause stated that 'no sales were to be made to any foreign merchants without the consent of both parties'. I wonder what prompted such xenophobia when the new partnership must have desperately needed customers of whatever nationality. Various clauses concerning the accounts followed, including one stating that no discounts were to be granted without both partners' consent. Another clause was included that I think was inserted primarily to please the young prospective partner: 'A horse to be kept for the partnership's use ... Riding expenses allowed.' Perhaps it was Mr Boult who, realising that his young partner would take advantage of that clause, insisted on the condition that followed: 'To be employed in the partnership's business only.' In fact, the whole agreement proclaims the inexperience and lack of business acumen of the parties involved.

In January 1778, less than a fortnight after the partnership was officially in operation, an accountant in Ashborn, who had been employed to compile the accounts for the previous year, wrote complaining that he was having great difficulty in sorting them out. He wrote, 'From the multitude of loose papers, I have collected a very imperfect state of your account that has been so long in agitation.' He complained that notes such as 'treacle overcharged' and 'overcharged in sugar' had been written on the books, and no other explanation had been given. Faced with the almost impossible task of sorting out the muddle, he concluded with the promise, 'When I receive your answer, the account shall be immediately settled.'[147] It must be admitted that even now, the documents that remain in the collection are confusing. For example one dated August 1778 claimed that the total owed by sundry debtors amounted to £802 16s 5d, while another claimed that in the same year, that total was £3,798 4s 10d.

I have been unable to find any documentary evidence as to what happened to the doomed refinery during the next decade. However, there are some papers dating from April 1797 that shed some light on the problem.[148] Seemingly, the complex had been let to Mr Hodson, a chandler, who had refused to pay his annual rent. Yet again, Mrs Hincks had enlisted the help of her lawyer Mr Richards. As there is no mention of Mr Boult or of the sugar house partnership, it would seem that sugar refining at Cuppings Street had been abandoned by that time.

Then in May 1797, Mr Hodson began to remove some of the fittings from the sugar house and to take down part of the building in order to make it more convenient for his needs. Mrs Hincks was horrified, and on 15 May, summoned her lawyer to deal with him. The lawyer immediately sent his clerk to interview Mr Hodson, but that did not deter him. Two days later, Mrs Hincks again got in touch with her lawyer, and begged him to go in person and threaten legal action against the chandler. Evidently, that had the desired effect and the tenant agreed to stop the demolition work. Although obviously the sugar house had been out of commission for some time, Mrs Hincks' great concern about the fittings suggests that she still harboured the hope that the sugar house might operate again in the future.

Mr Hodson continued to occupy the sugar house for the next few years. Then sometime in 1807 or early 1808, there was a disastrous fire in the building. Of course, sugar houses that were in operation were very prone to catching fire, but this fire aroused suspicion. Mr Richards, the lawyer, was enlisted to help negotiate the best terms with the insurance company, and recorded very many attendances on Mrs Hincks, Mr Hodson, and Mr Parry – presumably the insurance agent. In the end, he was successful in obtaining a promise from the insurers that they would give Mrs Hincks sufficient money to restore the premises 'as nearly as valuable as they were before'. That meant that the sugar house could be rebuilt and Mrs Hincks could continue her struggle to restore its fortunes. The rebuilding took place, and it was equipped with three pans for refining sugar and all the other necessary utensils. However, no new partnership agreement was drawn up, and it is doubtful whether the new sugar house was ever put into use.

By 1817, it was no longer in the hands of Mrs Hincks. By then her son Thomas Cowper Hincks, who then lived in Somerset Street, Marlebone, Middlesex, was responsible for the property and he decided that it should be sold, ostensibly as an on-going concern. The lawyers drew up an advertisement for the Liverpool and Chester newspapers at a cost of £3 11s declaring that the business 'has been and may be carried on to considerable extent and advantage in the City of Chester and its neighbourhood'. The advertisement stated that it was 'late the property of John Hincks deceased',[149] a fact that was expected to impress any prospective buyer, as the Hincks family were well known in the area despite the fact that John Hicks had been dead for almost fifty years. The 'spacious yard with warehouses, stables', a garden, and 'other suitable conveniences adjoining to the house' were to be included in the sale. The agent then included a suggestion that revealed exactly how desperate the owner must have been to conclude a sale: 'A part of the money may remain in the purchaser's hands upon proper security if desired.' Finally, if that inducement failed to attract a buyer and no offers were received, the lawyer was authorised to let the complex once again.

That is what actually happened. No buyer came forward for the business, and in 1818, it was decided to lease the property to the Gas Light Company. There was a period of hard bargaining, and as a result, the lawyer charged the family £5 5s for the 'very many attendances' on the Gas Light Company, Mr Hodson, the tenant who possibly wanted to renew his lease, Mr Joseph Hincks, a relative who represented Thomas Cowper Hincks, and on the printers. Despite having found a reliable tenant, Thomas was still hoping to sell his property in Cuppings Street,

Map showing the location of Chester Gas Works on the site of Hincks' refinery. (*Reproduced by kind permission of the chief archivist for Cheshire County Record Office. Ref: xxxviii/11-22 Town Plan 1875*)

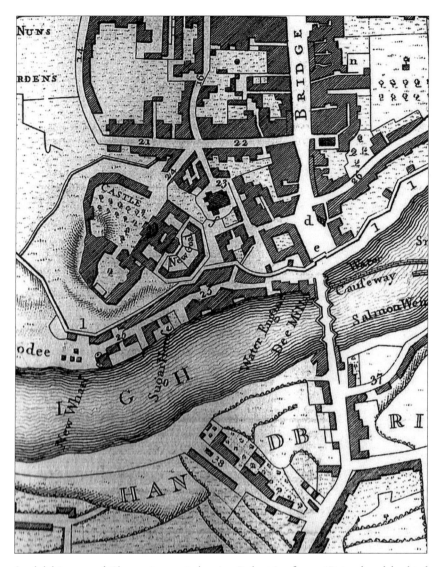

Stockdale's map of Chester in 1796 showing Roberts' refinery. (*Reproduced by kind permission of the principal archivist for Cheshire County Record Office Reference No.PM 14/120*)

for when he made his will in 1819, he left instructions that if it was sold during his lifetime, the money was to go to his son John. However, that did not happen. In 1875, Chester Gas Works were still located in Cuppings Street, where they continued to operate for many years.

However, there was one sugar refinery that was a success in Chester

Chester Castle and Skinner's Yard in the early nineteenth century by Francis Nicholson. One of the chimneys belching smoke would belong to the Roberts' refinery. (*Copyright Grosvenor Museum, Cheshire West and Chester Council*)

The site of the Roberts' refinery today. The site was cleared and made into a riverside park in 1930.

during the closing years of the eighteenth century. This small refinery was on the banks of the River Dee, immediately south of the castle between Skinners Lane and the river. It was built in a very convenient position where both the hogsheads of raw sugar and the coal for the furnaces, possibly from Neston on the Wirral, could be unloaded directly into the sugar house from barges. The refinery was owned by the Roberts family, who originally had been in the grocery business.[150] Apparently, there were two brothers; Thomas, who was named after his father, and John, who was made a freeman of the city in 1804. When Thomas Roberts died in 1815, he left the refinery and all his adjacent property on Skinners Lane to his wife Martha, but I have found no documents to chart the refinery's history after that date.

The later history of the Henthorne refinery is also lost, but as it is not recorded on the maps of 1800, it probably closed in the mid-eighteenth century.[151] The tragedies of Joseph Manesty's bankruptcy and the deaths of his two partners so soon afterwards spelt disaster for the other Chester refinery, despite the determined efforts of the stubborn Arabella to restore its fortunes. The Roberts' sugar house was the only Chester refinery to remain operational into the nineteenth century, and that was a very small concern.

Many factors contributed to this contraction of sugar refining in Chester. The competition from the Liverpool refiners was too strong. Their refineries were situated close to the docks where the raw sugar arrived, and so had a great advantage over those who had to transport the sugar miles inland or wait for a convenient high tide to allow access to the port of Chester. If the River Dee had remained navigable for ocean-going ships in the late eighteenth century, the history of the Chester sugar industry would have been very different. No entrepreneur came forward who had sufficient money or incentive to improve access to the sea. Dogged determination to continue was not enough, and so the industry succumbed to its competitors.

CHAPTER 4

Refineries in the South of the Region: Ormskirk, North Meols, Preston, Warrington, and Manchester

During the early development of the industry, many links can be traced between the various refiners, especially in the southern part of the region. Perhaps one of the earliest was forged by John Woosey, the refiner who, as we have seen, was trained in Liverpool before working in both Ormskirk and Chester. He was instrumental in the foundation of a sugar refinery in the small township of Bickerstaffe in the parish of Ormskirk.

It seems strange that Ormskirk should have been chosen as the site for a refinery, for the town was almost surrounded by moss lands. We have the evidence of the great traveller Celia Fiennes, who avoided the town in 1698 and explained, '… Passed by a mere or lake of water, there are many of these here about, but not going through Ormskirk I avoided going by … Martin Mere … it being very hazardous for strangers to pass by it.'[152] If the town was so inaccessible, why had a sugar refinery that needed transport for carrying both the raw materials to its base and the finished product to its customers been established there?

Nevertheless, in 1676 sugar refining was established in Ormskirk, 12 miles inland from the emerging port of Liverpool. Although the trade only continued in the township for a very short time, the fact that it was established at such an early date in that location is incredible. Transporting the hogsheads of raw sugar along the often waterlogged roadways of south-west Lancashire must have been an almost insurmountable problem. However, there were coal pits nearby to provide fuel for the boilers, and the weekly market provided a convenient outlet for the sugar.

Certainly sugar was in great demand in the town, for when Peter Sankey, the local mercer, died in 1613, the appraisers listed in their inventory of his goods:

1 lb 3oz of comfetts: 19d
1 lb of brown candy: 16d
1.5 lb of white candy: 3s
31.5 lb of sugar: 15d 39s 4d
3 score and 18 lb of treacle: 3d 19s 6d
9 lb of powder sugar: 4s 6d

These products were in the shop long before refineries were established in the north of England, so all these sugars and sugar products must have been produced in London and transported by ship around the coast. Sankey's will was dated before the planting of the large West Indian cane fields that catered later for the English market, so the sugar must have been expensive. In fact, an estimation of its value can be made by comparing its price to the 12d per week that was frequently granted to needy people during the seventeenth century by the Quarter Sessions. The court considered that amount to be sufficient to provide them with the necessities of life.[153] Thus, sugar at 15d per lb was a luxury, and yet the mercer in Ormskirk expected to sell large quantities of it. The local demand for sugar continued late into the seventeenth century, for as we have seen, James Berry, a grocer in Ormskirk, also carried large quantities of sugar and treacle. In 1686, his inventory listed: 2 lb treacle, 3 lb Barbados treacle, 20 lb brown bastard sugar, 2 lb white powdered sugar, and 2 lb bottoms of casks of bastard sugar.[154]

Henry Barton, an innkeeper in Ormskirk, recognised the possibility of making a great profit from this demand for sugar. In 1676, he proposed establishing a sugar refinery in Ormskirk, and contacted the skilled sugar boiler John Woosey, son of Henry Woosey, another innkeeper from Four Lane Ends in Bickerstaffe.[155] Barton proposed that Woosey, who as we know had been trained at the Liverpool sugar house of Danvers and Cleveland, should join him in the project. However, although Woosey was interested in the scheme to 'exercise the art, mystery, or occupation of sugar boyling and baking' in the town,[156] he insisted that a formal agreement should be drawn up before he would consider taking part

The cottages at Four Lane Ends in Bickerstaffe, the site of the cottage where John Woosey refined sugar in 1676.

in it. Henry Barton agreed and arranged a conference at his house to be attended by Margaret his wife, John Woosey, and Margaret's mother Jane Laithwaite, the widow of James Laithwaite, yet another innkeeper. It seems likely that Jane was included in the meeting in the hope that she would supply some of the funds that would be needed for the refinery. For his part, John Woosey brought along his father Henry and his friend Thomas Lyon, a clay potter, to support him in the discussion that followed.

Eventually after long negotiations, an agreement was reached. The Bartons and Jane Laithwaite 'would furnish [Woosey] with a house made fit and convenient for carrying on the work of sugar baking and boyling, and also should furnish [him] with sugar, fire, moulds, and all other materials needful for such laborious and toylesome workmanship for and during the term of seven years.' In return, Woosey undertook to hire any additional labour that was needed at his own cost. A significant part of the agreement was that 'at every year's end', all the profits would be divided into two equal halves. Woosey was to have one part and the innkeeper and his family were to have the other. Unfortunately, this clause was to lead to a bitter confrontation between the partners.

At first however, all went well. Henry and Jane agreed with Richard Bannastre, an agent, to negotiate for their supplies of raw sugar with Mr Clayton, a Liverpool merchant and specialist in the sugar trade. He agreed to supply them with a butt of raw sugar for £16. Then, the Barton family gave John £20 to cover the cost of that sugar, and ordered him to spend the remaining £4 on sugar moulds and 'such other instruments and tools as were necessary and requisite for the management of the said work'. Obviously, £4 was not sufficient to equip even a small sugar refinery, so John asked the partners for more money for the various instruments and tools that they had agreed to supply at the original conference. The family met and after some discussion, Margaret sent him 20s with the instructions that, 'In case the same did not suffice,' he should borrow whatever money he needed to equip the refinery, then production could begin as soon as possible. John must have shown some reluctance to get into debt. Yet Margaret gave him the firm undertaking that the three other partners would 'take care to discharge and pay off the same'.

Meanwhile, John persuaded his father Henry and his brother James to help him to transport the hogshead of sugar from the docks. They took Henry's cart and team of horses into Liverpool, loaded the huge butt onto the cart, and trundled it back to Ormskirk. The family's assistance must have saved the new partnership a considerable amount, because the cost of carting a hogshead of sugar the 12 miles to Ormskirk, would have been very high. Some idea of the cost can be gained from the Liverpool directory of 1790, which quoted the prices that the 'car men' – carters – were charging at that time. The cost was 4d for carting each hogshead of sugar not less than 8 cwt, and not more than 19 cwt any distance under 600 yards, and for carting the same weight between 600 and 1,200 yards the charge was 6d. At the earlier date, the cost of employing the 'car men' for the distance of 12 miles would have been immense.

Despite all their efforts, John could not start work, for the building that the Laithwaite-Barton family had promised to provide to be the sugar house was not ready for use. They claimed that they had been disappointed by their workmen, but there seems to have been some doubt about that, for at the later trial it was said that they 'pretended' to have had trouble with their workmen. However, their claim may have

The site of the proposed sugar house at Moor Street End in Ormskirk.

been true, for in her testimony at the ensuing court case, Anne Whalley, whose father was Jane Laithwaite's tenant, said that her father had been given notice to move out of the house because it was needed for a new sugar house. A fortnight later, her family had vacated the house, and so it had been ready for any alterations that were considered necessary. Thus, it is unclear as to who exactly was responsible for the delay in converting the property. Unfortunately, it is also impossible to identify the exact site of the cottage known as Daniel Sefton's, but as it was situated at Moor Street End, it was probably in the vicinity of the present bus station.

The partners were so anxious to start on their (hopefully very profitable) undertaking that they 'entreated and prevailed upon' Henry Woosey to allow his son to boil the sugar in the 'sope pan' at his home in Bickerstaffe. Presumably, Henry was also a soap boiler, and either had a spare boiler or had abandoned the trade, and so could allow his son to use his equipment. Finally, it was agreed that Margaret Barton should pay Henry some rent for the use of his premises and his equipment, and at last John was able to set to work. He boiled the sugar in the soap pan in his father's kitchen, and stood the sugar moulds full of drying sugar in the adjoining room. When everything was under way, Margaret Barton went to the new 'refinery' and gave John's mother another 20*s* for him. She sent the message that, 'Nothing should be wanting for his supply,' and asked his mother to encourage him to continue producing fine sugar, 'Fit for sale or to be made use of for any purpose.'

However, when the innkeeper and his family watched John at work and saw how easy it seemed to be to produce refined sugar, they decided that they had made a big mistake in sharing the profits equally with John. They felt that they deserved a larger portion for their investment and demanded that as an additional part to their agreement, John should teach Henry Barton the 'art of sugar baking and boyling'. They declared that unless he promised to train Henry, they would not provide him with the materials and necessary utensils as they had contracted to do at their original conference. In fact, they refused to honour their part of the agreement unless he met their new conditions. John was absolutely horrified at the proposal that he should pass on the skills he had spent many years acquiring without any recompense. His father Henry was also extremely annoyed, and explained that it had cost him a great deal of money, which he could ill-afford, to pay for his son's apprenticeship. In fact, he declared that John must not teach anyone the trade unless they paid at least £500 for their training – presumably that was the amount that he had spent on his son's apprenticeship. Then, as a sign of his anger at the unfair proposition, he declared that despite the rent he would lose, he would allow neither John nor his partners to use his house and equipment in future.

However, John did not stop the process immediately. Instead, he tried to placate the Bartons by suggesting that the family should sell the sugar he had already refined. Then, with the money they could provide him with premises and more stock, so that the work could continue as they had agreed originally. Of course, that meant that they would all forfeit their first profits, but at least the refining could continue. They remained adamant and would not proceed any further unless he agreed to train Henry Barton. John, backed by his father, stood firm and refused to train his partner.

Then, as an impasse had been reached, John stopped melting the raw sugar, and although some sugar was already melted, did not finish the process. Eventually about two months later, John made yet another attempt to resolve the dispute. He persuaded a friend of his to meet Jane Laithwaite and Henry Barton and take a parcel of the half-refined sugar

Lancaster Gaol from an old print.

for them. John sent the message that, unless the family provided him with a stove, he could not finish the refining or produce any more fine sugar. They stubbornly refused to accept the sugar, and told him to do what he liked with it; the family were determined that they would not finance him any longer. When this final attempt at reconciliation failed, John left Bickerstaffe and moved to Chester to work as a labourer in Mr Henthorne's refinery for two years in 1677 and 1678.[157]

The family were not content to leave the matter there. They went to court and obtained an order against John for debt, demanding the return of all the money that according to their agreement, they had given him to finance the venture. Of course, he was unable to pay back the money that he had spent on the butt of raw sugar and on all the equipment, and that as manager, he had bought for the new refining project. Consequently, they committed him to gaol as a debtor, and not content with that, they made certain that he would not be allowed bail unless he provided a large amount of money, much more than he could possibly find, as a surety. Consequently, John remained incarcerated in gaol until he finally managed to arrange a trial at the assizes. There no doubt, he received justice and freedom. Unfortunately, the details of the verdict are not available.

After that fiasco, there was no more sugar refining in Ormskirk until the years of the Second World War, when sugar products were manufactured in a Nissan hut in Wigan Road near the Ropers Arms on the site of Jones' rope walk. This business too did not survive for long, but ended in the early years of the 1950s – well beyond the time scale of this study.

North Meols and Preston

North Meols' earliest connection with the sugar trade occurred when an Irish ship carrying sugar was wrecked on a bank near the Old Pool in 1565. Since then, local tradition has identified the site of the wreck as the long bank near the centre of Churchtown known as Sugar Hillock, where No. 18 Sunny Road stands today.[158] Although the site is some distance from the coast, that does not disprove the tradition, for many acres of land in the area have been reclaimed from the sea since that time.

The first documentary evidence of the possible existence of a sugar refinery in the area comes from a map of the Ribble Estuary surveyed by Samuel Fearon and John Eyes in 1736-1737. The survey was dedicated to Sir Thomas Lowther and Roger Hesketh Esquire of North Meols, and various landmarks were named along the coastline, one of which was 'Sugar Houses'. It is difficult to pinpoint the site on modern maps because so much of the marshland has been drained, and consequently altered the coastline. However, on the Tithe map the New Inn is shown on approximately the same site, which could indicate that the sugar houses developed into a distillery with an associated inn, although that is mere speculation.[159]

Today, a small cluster of whitewashed cottages stands near the site of the inn, which was demolished soon after the Second World War. One of these in Bank Nook, off Radnor Drive, bears the name of 'Sugar House Cottage'. The owner told me that it was built about 1740, but beyond that she could not explain how it came to have that name. It is far too small to have been the original sugar house, but it could have been one of the cottages built to house the sugar boiler or one of the other workers on the site. Bowen, another surveyor, also marked the sugar houses of

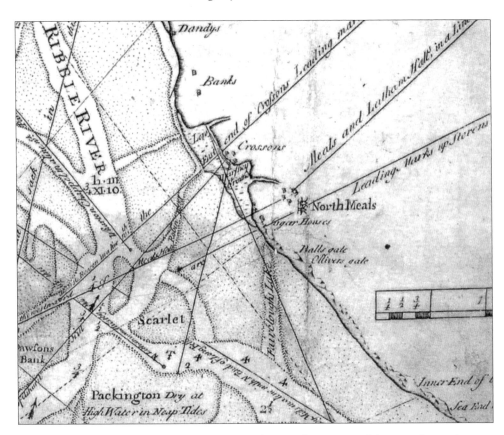

Fearon and Eyes map of the Ribble estuary showing the position of the sugar houses in North Meols. (*Reproduced by kind permission of Andrew White at Lancaster Maritime Museum*)

North Meols on his map of Lancashire in 1752. Evidently, at that date the buildings were thought to be so important that they warranted the same size of print on the map as the market town of Ormskirk, and yet I can find no further definite documentary evidence to support the existence of the refinery at that time.

The 1736 map also shows a stream flowing into the Ribble Estuary to the east of the sugar houses, from where the watercourse fed into a deeper area of water in the estuary known as 'Fairclough's Lake'.[160] This lake was 2 miles long and 0.5 miles wide where it flowed into the open sea. It narrowed towards the landward side and was recorded on various charts as being between 4 and 7 fathoms deep.[161] Therefore, small ships were able to dock in the deeper water of this lake before the channel of

Sugar House Cottage, Bank Nook off Radnor Drive.

the Ribble approaching Preston was deepened. It is possible that some of those ships carried sugar, and that their cargoes were unloaded into small warehouses that were known as sugar houses, or perhaps that was indeed the name of a small refinery complex that was established to process the sugar.[162] Certainly one grocer, who lived at Formby, at the other side of what has now become Southport, had a large stock of sugar. His inventory made in 1674 listed 13 lb of loaf sugar, 3.75 lb of powdered sugar, 3.75 lb of sugar candy, and an unbelievable 300 lb of molasses.[163] Perhaps that molasses was the product of the sugar houses at North Meols, a few miles further up the coast.

Peter White, a sea captain from Wicklow, frequently docked at Fairclough's Lake in the early years of the eighteenth century. He knew Nicholas Blundell and often stayed at his house. On 30 March 1710, Nicholas and his wife met the captain at North Meols, and after dining at Mr Rimmer's inn, the party went aboard the *Betty* on Fairclough's lake.[164] Unfortunately, there is no mention of the cargo of the *Betty* in the diary and the editor of the diary Frank Tyrer was unable to find out whether Peter White traded with the West Indies or only with Ireland. However, there was a ship called the *Betty* recorded on 13 June 1712 sailing to Lancaster carrying a mixed cargo, including one hogshead, three barrels of sugar, and two bags of ginger. This suggests that the *Betty* did engage in transatlantic trade.[165] If so, perhaps Nicholas had an interest in the sugar trade and followed the tradition set by his grandfather William, who it will be remembered, was involved in early transatlantic trading with the West Indies. Could the sugar houses in North Meols have been the warehouses used by those early importers? Did they set up early refineries on the Ribble Estuary at the same time as Danvers and Cleveland built their first refinery on the banks of the Mersey? Perhaps one day some documents will be found to support my speculations.

There may have been some connection with the Hesketh family from Warrington, a family that had many relatives in the district. When John Hesketh of Warrington, described as a gentleman, died in 1767, he left money to forty poor householders in Marshside, North Meols. His sons Robert and William were executors of his will,[166] and a Robert Hesketh, who acted as a merchant in Chester, was deeply involved at that time with the Warrington sugar refinery. It is tempting to speculate that the Marshside sugar houses had belonged to John Hesketh. As Fairclough's Lake silted up, they could no longer import the sugar to Marshside, and so the sugar houses were abandoned, leaving the workers in need – a need met by John in his will. Meanwhile, his son continued the family interest in refining by joining the partnership of the Warrington refinery. Of course, that is all merely a speculation; I lack definite proof.

Preston

Preston too presents many problems, for although there is evidence that there was a sugar refinery in the town in 1754, it does not appear on any maps, nor is it included in any directory. Angerstein, a Swede who travelled around England and Wales making notes in his diary about various industrial sites, wrote, 'As well as the textile mills, there is a sugar refinery in the town, and also a melting furnace in a foundry making many kinds of castings, but I was there on a Sunday and it was not working.'[167] The only slight clue to the possible owner of the refinery is the fact that the sugar baker William Farrer moved to Preston from Liverpool and died there in 1795. However, he was still working in Liverpool until the 1780s, so it is unlikely that he had established a sugar refinery in Preston in the 1750s. It is possible that the Preston refinery worked in collaboration with the sugar houses at the mouth of the Ribble Estuary at North Meols, refining sugar that had been landed where the channel was deeper. Again, we need more definite proof.

Warrington

The establishment of sugar refining in Warrington was the direct result of improvements to the River Mersey made at the end of the seventeenth century. Before that time, merchants in southern Lancashire had great difficulty in transporting their supplies to and from the port of Liverpool across the mosslands of the area. The only solution to their problems was to clear and deepen the Mersey and the Irwell and so allow small boats to reach Warrington and Manchester, but that was a huge undertaking requiring a great deal of capital, and more importantly, permission from Parliament. Nevertheless, they decided to attempt the project, and in the 1660s, they presented a Bill to Parliament to make the two rivers navigable. Their hopes were dashed when it was defeated by the landed interest.

Notwithstanding this setback, Thomas Patten of Warrington (1662-1726), a tobacco and sugar merchant, decided to continue the campaign to improve the rivers. He had always bought his refined sugar in Liverpool, and then experienced great difficulties as he struggled to transport it back to Warrington in carts along roads that were often water logged. He realised that if only the old fish weirs between Runcorn and Warrington were removed, small boats carrying his supplies would be able to sail up the Mersey as far as Warrington. With this in view, he financed a scheme to clear the river. It was such a success that he was able to claim in a letter to Richard Norris in 1698 that, 'There have been sent to Liverpool and from Liverpool 2,000 tons of goods a year.'[168] However, that was not the end of the problem, for many goods had to be transported further inland to Manchester and beyond. Encouraged by his success, Patten planned to improve the river further upstream, but that could not be done until the Mersey and Irwell Act was finally passed by Parliament in 1721. Even then, it was not was possible to make the rivers fully navigable as far as Manchester until 1739.

The long delay did not prevent the Warrington merchants from taking full advantage of the newly cleared waterway as far as their town. Patten built Bank Quay, with several warehouses to store his own goods and also to act as a distribution point for many of the metal goods made in the district by other companies with which he was involved. Then, he decided that instead of buying refined sugar in Liverpool, it would be more profitable to buy unrefined sugar from the sugar merchants and process it in Warrington; he had the boats to bring the hogsheads up the river, and he had a site for the refinery. Also, the coal to fuel the boilers was available nearby. Consequently, he began to construct his sugar house complex, which was completed about 1717. Many of the other traders in Warrington also profited from the early dock developments, and were able to expand their works. In fact, when Defoe visited the area in the mid-1720s, he commented that the copper and sugar works, the pin works, and the making of sail cloth were well established in the town.[169]

The Patten family was also involved in the copper works in Warrington, where from the middle years of the eighteenth century, copper boilers were produced for export to the West Indies for use in boiling raw sugar and distilling rum. At the same works currency bangles and various copper trinkets were made for sale to the natives in Africa in exchange for slaves.[170]

The Patten family also prospered through their connections with the various aspects of the sugar trade, and as very astute business men, were always ready to take advantage of conditions in the market. For instance as we have seen, in a letter sent by Joseph Manesty, a sugar merchant, to his partner in the Chester refinery in 1758, he remarked that, 'Mr Patten bought ordinary Jamaicas last week at 40s.' That seemed to be a very high price for a hogshead of molasses. However, in the next letter we read, 'All the Jamaica fleet for London & Bristol are lost or taken but one.' Thus, the younger Thomas Patten had gambled that the price of Jamaican sugar would rise, and he had been proved to be correct. The ships had been lost as a result of the Seven Years War, and Jamaican sugar was virtually unobtainable.[171]

In 1750, Patten built Bank Hall to be his residence, which at that time stood among open fields overlooking the Mersey.[172] This grand residence was a visible expression both of the family's wealth and of

Bank Quay from Donbavand's painting of 1772 (*Reproduced courtesy of Warrington Borough Council – Libraries, Heritage and Learning*)

Bank Quay today.

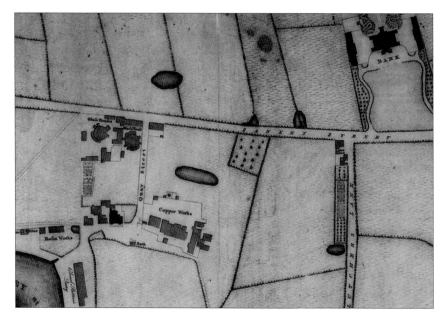

A plan of Bank Quay showing the copper works and Bank Hall top right. (*Reproduced courtesy of Warrington Borough Council – Libraries, Heritage and Learning*)

their contribution to the development of Warrington. Indeed in 1755, the family's sugar refinery was acknowledged to be one of the leading industries in the town by Chamberlayne.[173]

Meanwhile, Patten had developed another sugar house complex near Horsemarket Street in the centre of Warrington. Exactly when this was built is unclear, but certainly Robert Hesketh, a merchant from Chester, bought all the equipment for this sugar house in 1768 from Thomas Marsden & Co. He paid the amazing sum of £938 18s 11d for nearly 10,000 utensils. A great number of these were made of copper – pans, moulds, ladles, and casks, possibly products of Patten's own copper works. The large copper coolers were bought for £125, while the millstone for grinding cost £23. The contents of the premises were listed floor by floor as the valuers progressed through the refinery,[174] and consequently, the inventory for the sale provides us with a reliable picture of the layout and organisation of a typical refinery at that time.

It was a large building with five floors and a garret that was used as a store room, where equipment was kept that was not currently in use. There were several thousand drips and moulds distributed around each

Bank Hall, originally the home of the Patten family, now Warrington Town Hall.

of the upper floors of the building, while on the ground floor were all the utensils used in the early processing of the molasses – the scum tub, the scum baskets, candy pots, candy mugs, treacle funnels, paddles, shovels, and many other utensils. Evidently, the upper floors housed rows upon rows of sugar moulds full of boiled sugar, which dripped impurities into the mugs that had been placed below them until it was judged that the process was complete and the sugar was pure. Meanwhile, the boiling took place on the ground floor. The twelve iron candlesticks listed among the contents of the ground floor presumably held the only lights in the working area. The process could not be allowed to stop until the boiling was complete, and so the men had to work through the hours of darkness. Of course, the fires under the boilers provided some light, but nevertheless, candles were needed for the clerks, who also worked during the long, dark hours of winter. No wonder there were so many catastrophic fires in the industry.

Where the original refinery was located is a complete mystery. There are three candidates for the origin of the inventory: two refineries in Chester and the one in Lancaster. It is possible that the equipment came from the Chester sugar house, which had once belonged to Henthorne, and had passed to Marsden – who employed John Blease – and which now Marsden had decided to sell. Certainly, Marsden was in business in 1758 according to a letter from Manesty to his partners in the Hincks Company. However, there is no definite proof that he took over from Henthorne, or that he decided to sell in 1768, although it seems very likely, for nothing is recorded about that refinery after that date. The fact that Robert Hesketh, one of the merchants involved in the sale, came from Chester, supports this theory, but of course there was another refinery in Chester.

As far as that other Chester refinery is concerned, one of the partners had died in 1767 – a year before the inventory was compiled – leaving instructions that his share of the sugar house had to be sold and that his partner had to have the first opportunity to buy the contents. However, the remaining partner in that Chester refinery continued the business in the 1770s, which suggests that he had bought his partner's share, and therefore the factory's contents had not reached the open market.

Then there is the possibility that Lancaster was the location for the 'inventory' factory. Thomas Marsden, who sold the equipment, was linked to the Lancaster sugar house in a letter written by Manesty to Wilson of the Chester sugar house in 1758, in which he wrote 'complyd with by Mr Marsden and Lancaster Sugar House'.[175] Of course, that reference could be interpreted to mean two different refineries, one in Lancaster and one in Chester. However, there was an advertisement for the sale of a sugar house in Lancaster in a local newspaper dated 30 June 1768, the year of the inventory. We know that the sugar boilers in Lancaster had built a new factory and had equipped it with new utensils, so perhaps they had decided to offer the old refinery for sale complete with all its fittings. This provides strong support for the Lancaster factory being the source of the equipment, but unfortunately, no reliable documentary evidence has survived to confirm that indeed that was the case. Thus, the real source of the inventory remains a mystery. Nevertheless, the facts illustrate how prosperous and confident the sugar industry was at that time.

It is interesting to read in the inventory that the moulds were made of copper, because elsewhere in Lancashire the moulds were being made of earthenware. Patten, who of course had an interest in the copper industry, must have introduced the use of metal moulds into his refinery, because unlike the earthenware ones, they would not break. Gradually, that idea was accepted by the industry, and by the nineteenth century most sugar moulds were made of metal – not by then of copper, but of steel.

Sometime during the intervening years, Thomas Patten took John Leigh of Oughtrington into partnership in the ownership of the sugar house complex near Horsemarket Street, but it would seem that he did not become involved in the actual administration of the business. Indeed, Robert Hesketh had continued to be concerned in the running of the business since the purchase of utensils in 1768. However in 1778, a completely new partnership was formed between Robert Hesketh, Joseph Parr, and Richard Astley, all described as merchants, and that partnership leased the sugar house and all the ancillary buildings from Thomas Patten and John Leigh.[176]

Once Parr had been included in the agreement to lease the sugar house complex in 1778, he borrowed money from Thomas Patten (£2,000) and John Leigh (£1,000). He also gave a bond for £1,250 to his mother, while Robert Hesketh and Joseph Jackson stood as guarantors.[177] All these transactions suggest that like John Baicklin in Liverpool, Parr was a skilled sugar boiler who was taken into partnership to assist the experienced, but elderly Robert Hesketh, and to ensure the smooth working of the factory. Nevertheless, the size of his investment – albeit in borrowed money – meant that he was probably the chief shareholder. In fact three years later, the firm became known as Joseph Parr & Co.

From the lease, we get some indication of the site and size of the sugar refinery complex. It describes the property as, 'Those two several sugar houses with warehouses and accompanying house, stable, shippon, and other outbuildings situate near Horsemarket Street.' A clearer picture of the area emerges from the map of the centre of Warrington drawn in 1772 by the surveyors Wallworth and Donbavand, where the sugar house is shown in detail near the horse market, bounded by Sugar House Lane and Riding Lane, which later became lost in Bewsey Street.

In 1781, there were many changes among the sugar boilers. For instance, Robert Hesketh decided to retire. A tripartite deed of dissolution

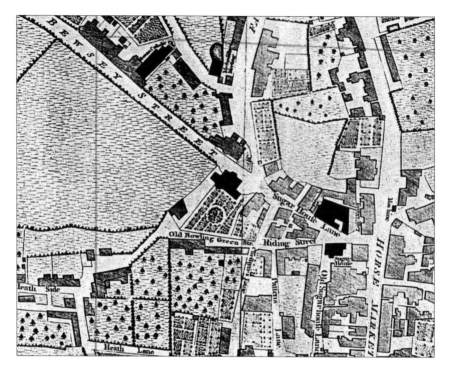

Wallwork & Donbavand's map of 1772 showing the position of the refinery in Sugar House Lane near the Horse Market. (*Reproduced by kind permission of the County Archivist Lancashire Record Office*)

was drawn up by which the partnership was dissolved, and for a short while, Joseph Parr took complete control of the sugar house. In the same year, he married Ellen Lyon and they moved away from Warrington to make their home in Fir Grove in West Derby. It may have been this move and the consequent lack of keen supervision that caused the profits of the refinery to decline, or there may have been other external factors that contributed to its losses. Certainly, the decline was clearly evident, for a revealing conversation is recorded between Thomas Lyon and William Turner, a solicitor, declaring, 'Joseph Parr has a trade which is leaving him and doing him no good.'

Nevertheless, Lyon and Turner recognised that Joseph was an astute business man, and so they proposed that he should be asked to establish a bank in Warrington. This was agreed, and the bank of Parr, Lyon, and Kerfoot, the forerunner of the well known Parr's Bank, later the Westminster Bank, was formed. Meanwhile, to assist Joseph's

Joseph Parr & Co.'s sugar house as it is today.

new venture, Richard Astley of the dissolved partnership promised to indemnify the sugar refinery company of Joseph Parr & Co from being called upon for any rent due upon the sugar house and utensils, which the company held by lease from the executors of Robert Patten, who had died in 1780. Thus, Joseph Parr was freed from any financial responsibility for the sugar house, and he was at liberty to pursue his new career while the refinery continued under the control of Richard Astley.

However, through his wife's family Joseph Parr was still connected with the sugar trade in Warrington, for John Lyon was now the owner of

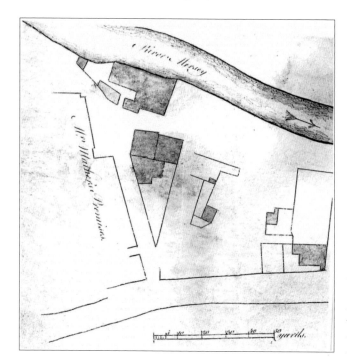

Plan of the site from Thomas Lyons lease. (*Reproduced courtesy of Warrington Borough Council – Libraries, Heritage and Learning*)

the sugar house at Bankey (Bank Quay) on the banks of the Mersey. This refinery was the original sugar house built by Patten in the early years of the eighteenth century. The lease was held by Thomas Lyon, who traded as Thomas Lyon & Co. Evidently, Patten had sold the whole sugar house estate on the banks of the Mersey to John Lyon, who then had built a completely new wharf called Lyons Quay at Bankfields. In 1781, John died and the sugar house complex, including the wharf, passed to his sister and her husband Walter Kerfoot, who as we have seen, was one of the partners with Thomas Lyon and Joseph Parr in the foundation of Parr's Bank.[178]

When the Kerfoots inherited the complex, Thomas Lyon's lease had to be renewed, and among other conditions, he had to undertake to keep the sugar house in good repair.[179] In addition to the sugar house, a coal house and a coal yard were included in the lease. No doubt the yard was used by coal merchants to store coal from the nearby pits, either for the use of the refinery or to await loading into barges for transport down to the port of Liverpool for use in the town, or else for export to Ireland or more distant places.

The common cart road that was protected by Walter Kerfoot and remains today as a right of way through the huge industrial complex now owned by Unilever.

Thomas, a true entrepreneur, realised the potential of the site that he had leased alongside the river and proposed developing it. However, Walter had some misgivings about the extent of the proposed new developments and felt it was necessary to include some restrictions in the lease to protect the site he owned. Consequently, he specified in the document the exact boundaries of the proposed buildings. Thomas could enclose only 'the vacant land at the end of the coal yard adjoining the river in a straight line 30 yards with the sugar house to the warehouse, called Rock Warehouse'. Walter realised that it was essential to retain some space immediately surrounding the sugar house to allow easy access both to the wharf and to the refinery for the wagons carrying the huge barrels of raw sugar. Therefore, he specified that the development had not to encroach nearer than 10 yards to the sugar house.

Another of his concerns was that the 'common cart road' from Warrington to Liverpool, which was immediately behind the site, be kept clear of any obstructions. Consequently, yet another clause was included in the lease, ruling that the cart road was to 'be in no way restricted'. If he obeyed all these conditions, then Thomas was free to develop the site in whatever way he wished.

All the vessels that used the wharves in Warrington had to pay the owners wharfage for the privilege, but as lease holder, Thomas was to be entitled to use the wharf free of charge for any goods destined for the sugar house, or for goods in transit from the refinery. However, he was warned in the lease not to allow any other goods 'from or out of any boat, flat, or vessel, or otherwise' to land at the quay without paying wharfage. The income from that source was to stay in Walter's hands. Thomas was granted another unusual privilege. He was promised the free use of Walter's crane to lift goods to or from the boats if his own crane was accidentally out of use for a short time. This would suggest that there had been some difficulties with the cranes on the quay, perhaps the ropes had broken or the chains had snapped. Whatever had happened, Thomas must have asked Walter to include this clause to guard against any similar 'temporary impediment' to the working of the refinery in the future.

Thomas was granted the lease for a surprising thousand years for a mere £60 per annum. Of course, I suppose the whole development project was regarded as a gamble in those early days, but with hindsight that lease was immensely valuable. Even at the time, the importance of all these developments for the people of Warrington was recognised. As Aikin declared in his book of 1795, 'The refinery of sugar and the making of glass have employed many hands.' Most of these 'hands' remain anonymous. In fact, only one sugar boiler appears in the lists of wills for Warrington, and that is George Robinson who died in 1781. He was in debt to Richard Astley when he died, which suggests that he was employed in the Horsemarket refinery. However, his assets must have been very small, for no one took the trouble to apply to administer the will until 1797, sixteen years after his death.

The Lyon family continued to be successful, despite the fact that there were always people ready to cheat them by various ingenious ways. For instance in 1810, the manager of the refinery sent this letter to Edward Connelly, a merchant who had sold them a quantity of molasses: 'In the Hope cargo of sugar, one hogshead of ours (intended for sugar) was entirely sand, of which we shall send you a sample by the first conveyance that you may recover it. We never before heard of such a thing and hope if there is a way to punish the person for such conduct you will do it. J. L. & Co.'[180]

Memories of sugar refining at the close of the eighteenth century in central Warrington were published in a Warrington newspaper in 1936. An elderly lady had recorded how as a child she watched the night time activity outside the Horsemarket refinery about the turn of the century. She describes:

> From her bedroom window in ... Tumber Alley she watched the thick, treacly molasses being delivered by carters from Liverpool to the sugar house. With old fashioned storm lamps or flares, they came in the gloom to the Sugar House yard, sweating horses straining at the girths, whips cracking, oaths, laughter and joking, the banging and rolling of barrels, cries of, 'Gee up,' 'Gee back,' and 'Whoa there, steady', loads taken off, empties taken on, and the transport over, by common consent an adjournment to the nearest tavern, where a tired drover might 'wet his whistle' to the tune of five pints for 1s with a copper over for a wisp of twist and a clay pipe.

This certainly brings to life the days of sugar refining in Warrington, days that were thought to be over by 1825, when it was reported that, 'The refining of sugar formerly carried on extensively no longer prevailed.'[181] However, that industry was to be resurrected not many miles away on the banks of the Sankey Canal later in the nineteenth century.

Manchester

Sugar refining in Manchester, like that in Warrington, could not be established until the Mersey and Irwell Navigation was opened in 1739.[182] As we have seen, until that time it was virtually impossible to transport the hogsheads of raw sugar from the port of Liverpool across the mosslands of south Lancashire to the town. Once that difficulty had been overcome and the heavy loads could be transported by water as far as Manchester, plans were made to build a sugar house on the southern bank of the Irwell. A site was chosen not far from the old quay, which was the furthest point of the navigable river until 1840. We do not know

Two etchings of the Manchester quayside in the early eighteenth century. The buildings with the chimneys to the rear of the warehouse in the first etching may have been an early sugar house complex. (*V. I. Tomlinson Early Warehouses on Manchester Waterways, TLCAS 66 1956 p. 59*)

when the refinery was actually opened, but it is possible that it was the large building with the many chimneys on an engraving of the old quay.

The first documentary evidence of the early sugar bakers in Manchester was a report in December 1757 about a tragedy that had occurred at one of the refineries. One of the workers was scalded to death in boiling sugar. A messenger was sent to fetch the coroner, who lived in Rochdale eight miles away. When he arrived, he examined the body and recorded the circumstances of the death on his expense account. He named the victim as Joacum Henry Sholt and describing him as a Dutchman. We do not know how he came to be working in Lancashire, but it is likely that he had learnt his trade in one of the refineries in Amsterdam and had come to Manchester to train local men to work in the sugar industry. It is yet another instance of a man coming from the European mainland to work in the refineries in Lancashire.

The first Manchester sugar baker to be named in a directory was Sam Norcot of Water Street near the old quay. His sugar house was a

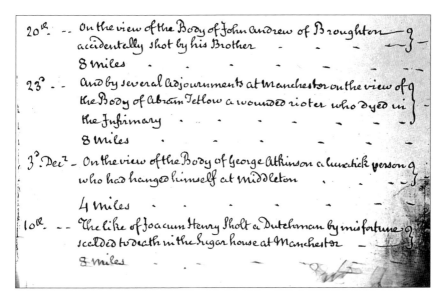

20ᵗ. -- On the view of the Body of John Andrew of Broughton
accidentally shot by his Brother   -   -   -   -
8 miles   .   .   .   -   -

23ᵗ. -- And by several Adjournments at Manchester on the view of
the Body of Abram Jetlow a wounded rioter who dyed in
the Infirmary   .   .   -   -   -
8 miles   .   .   -

3ᵗ Decᵗ -- On the view of the Body of George Atkinson a lunatick person
who had hanged himself at Middleton   .   -
4 miles   .   .   -   -   -

10ᵗ. -- The like of Joacum Henry Sholt a Dutchman by misfortune
scalded to death in the Sugar house at Manchester   -
8 miles   -   .   -   -

The Coroner's report of the Dutchman scalded to death in a sugar vat. (*Reproduced by kind permission of the County Archivist at Lancashire Record Office Ref: QSP 1758/9*)

tall building built gable end to the river so that barrels could be loaded onto any floor in the house directly from it.[183] Sam Norcot must have been well respected among his contemporaries in the trade, for as we have seen, Arabella Hincks of Chester sought his advice when her husband died, leaving her with an ailing sugar refining business. His letter demonstrated that he had an intimate knowledge of the industry and could identify the possibility of making economies, and so possibly rescuing the Chester sugar house.

Thomas Rothwell, Norcot's clerk, was also listed in the Manchester and Salford Directory of 1773. Mary, Sam Norcot's mother, described Thomas as her nephew in her will proved in 1787, and so it would seem that the refinery was a family business, in common with so many of the early refineries. However by the time of the will, Thomas had left the refinery and was working as a dyer. It is significant that, although the sugar house is marked on C. Laurent's map of 1793, there is no sugar house on the map completed the following year by William Green, and the words 'Dye Works' are printed over the site of the whole complex.[184] Seemingly, by then the premises had been converted into a dye works – possibly by Thomas Rothwell – to cater for the burgeoning trade in cotton manufacturing in the town. This can have happened only shortly before Green's map was published, for in her will, Mary stated, 'The most considerable part of my personal estate [was] engaged in the co-partnership trade wherein I am partner and which is carried on under the firm of The Manchester Sugar baking Company.' She declared that her investment would 'continue to be so employed for the now remainder of a term of seven years'. She specified that certain bequests were not to be paid until that term expired. It would seem that as soon as that term had expired, the sugar house had been converted for use in the more lucrative trade of dyeing.

Several Liverpool merchants, including the sugar baker Charles Woods, planned to build a quay on the Salford side of the Irwell. Among the other promoters were Henry Rauthmell and John Okill, both of whom had family connections with Liverpool refiners. Of course, their main purpose was to facilitate the shipment of goods to the Manchester area. However, it seems very likely that the partners, who all had connections with the sugar industry, also intended to erect a sugar house on that side of the river to compete with the Manchester Sugar Baking Company. Land was bought in 1755, an open quay was built, and the first warehouse was erected at right angles to the river.[185] In May 1762, they entered into partnership with the Duke of Bridgewater, who also owned land alongside the river. However, the Duke wisely bought three quarters of the shares to prevent any competition to his interests in Manchester developing on the Salford side the river. Then in December 1779, he extended his holding by buying the remaining thirty shares off his seven partners, thus eliminating any influence the Liverpool men may have had on the development of Salford Quay.[186]

Once the Irwell had been made navigable to Hunts Bank in the 1840s, the Salford bank of the river became the site of another sugar refinery. This belonged to Sharp and Galloway, whose Cannon Street works were described as being in Chapel Street, Salford, in the directory of 1869. Another refinery was established by Binyon and Shapland in Chester Street, later becoming Fryer, Benson, and Forsters by 1869.[187] Thus, sugar refining moved away from its original home on Water Street, but it still had a presence in mid-nineteenth century Manchester.

One building that did remain in Water Street was the public house, where the workers slaked their thirst after working long hours in the overheated atmosphere of the sugar house. In 1781, it was called The Sugar Loaf and the landlord was Richard Catterall.[188] He remained in charge of the pub at No. 87 and 89 Water Street for the next fourteen years. By 1869 the old pub was still there, but by then the name had changed slightly to The Three Sugar Loaves. It is strange that signs on public houses often record industries that had moved away from the district many years ago.

CHAPTER 5

Sugar Refining in Lancaster and Whitehaven

We are very fortunate in having a first hand account of the life of John Hodgson, Lancaster's earliest sugar refiner, written by his apprentice William Stout.[189] According to Stout, Hodgson, who was born in Ellel, 6 miles south of Lancaster, was apprenticed to John Greenwood of Lancaster, a grocer and apothecary, and was married twice. No doubt his first wife, a member of the Wilson family of Dallam Tower then in Westmorland, brought a substantial dowry to the marriage, but she died soon after the birth of their son Thomas. His second wife was Isabel Hodgson of Lancaster, whose brother was employed as a merchant in both York and Hull. This brother introduced Hodgson to overseas trade and together they bought a Dutch prize ship in which they imported both wine from France and tobacco from Virginia during the 1670s. In fact, Stout claimed that the first voyage from Lancaster to America was made under the auspices of John Hodgson. Their successful ventures brought wealth to the family, and in 1681, Hodgson was made a magistrate. In 1684, 1688, and 1701 he served as mayor of Lancaster, despite the fact that as a Quaker, he was legally barred from such offices by the Corporation Act of 1661. However, there appears to have been a 'considerable amount of complicity between friends and the town's establishment in order to prevent the question of the oaths being raised'.[190]

Through his interest in the wine trade, Hodgson became interested in distilling and decided to build a sugar house in Lancaster to produce molasses for the distillery that he planned to establish in the town.

Thus, the initial motives for the birth of the sugar refining industry in Lancaster differed completely from those in Liverpool, Whitehaven, or Warrington. Since Hodgson had no knowledge of the trade, he brought both refiners and distillers from London and Bristol, who understood 'the art and mystery of it', to work for him. Stout made the characteristically pessimistic comment that they 'kept him [Hodgson] in ignorance of the mystery, so that it was supposed he suffered loss'. Despite the fact that raw sugar was not imported directly into Lancaster at that time, Hodgson was determined to overcome all the problems and arranged to import the raw material through Liverpool and transport it from there in coastal vessels.

It was this difficulty that initiated his partnership with John Lawson, a merchant of Lancaster, who was a fellow Quaker. Lawson lived in St Leonardsgate, where he had provided a refuge for George Fox in 1652. As Fox recorded in his journal, 'I went to the steeple house at Lancaster … But they haled me out and stoned me along the street till I came to John Lawson's house.'[191] Lawson himself suffered for his faith, being imprisoned in 1654 for speaking in Lancaster Parish Church, and being dismissed in 1668 from the office of bailiff of the customs for refusing to take the oath as required by the Corporation Act of 1661. Altogether, he spent a year in jail and was fined a total of £200 as a result of his beliefs as a Quaker. Nevertheless, he was a successful merchant, and it was his business acumen that attracted John Hodgson to seek a partnership with him.

In 1679, Lawson built a stone bridge – later to be known as Merchant's Bridge – from the bottom of the garden of his house in St Leonardsgate over a mill stream, in order to provide access to the Green Ayre alongside the River Lune. Then a year later, he was given permission to erect a wharf 20 yards long and also to build a crane on the Green Ayre. Freemen of Lancaster were allowed to use this wharf if they paid Lawson 4d for each ton of merchandise that they transported.[192] This became known as Lawson's Quay and was the first of a series of wharves that were built upstream from the old bridge. Whether this development was made as a result of the proposed sugar house, or whether it was all in place before the decision was made to build the refinery and distillery, is uncertain. However, it proved to be a great asset when the new complex, built in the grounds of John Lawson's house, became operational in the early

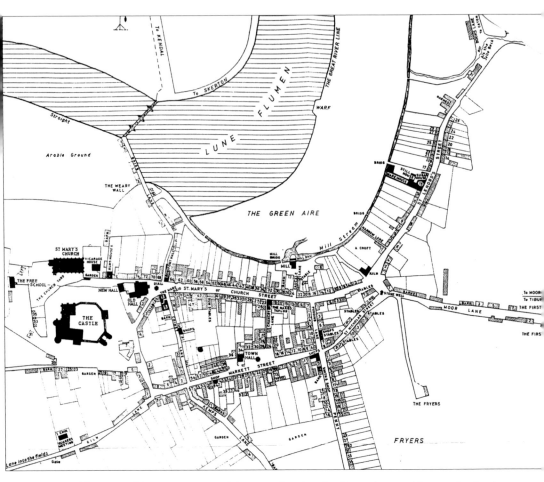

The map of Lancaster surveyed in 1684 showing the Green Ayre and Lawson's wharf.
(*This map was found in the basement of Town Hall in Burnley in 1952. I am indebted
to Andrew White of the Lancaster Museum Service for the original illustrations in this
chapter*)

1680s. Later, ships from the West Indies could dock close to the refinery
that was on the other side of the mill stream, and unload the hogsheads
of sugar into the warehouses ready for processing. Thus, the foundations
were laid for an industry that was to provide employment for Lancaster's
workforce until the beginning of the nineteenth century.

In addition to their involvement in the sugar refinery, both Hodgson
and Lawson continued in business as retailers during the 1680s. In fact,
John Hodgson is recorded in the Corporation Minute Book as paying
stallage in 1685,[193] so although he was a very successful merchant, an

established sugar refiner, and an ex-mayor, he continued to pay for a stall in Lancaster market where his apprentices would sell groceries, including no doubt, sugar from his refinery. The shortage of coins of small value was a difficulty suffered by most retailers during the second half of the seventeenth century, and many resorted to issuing their own token coins. In fact several, including one issued in 1669 by Robert Barker, a grocer of Lancaster, featured sugar loaves on the obverse side of the coin, a sign of the importance attached to the product in the town at that time. Both Hodgson and Lawson also issued their own tokens. Hodgson's featured an angel with a sword, while the obverse side of Lawson's farthing depicted what appears to be a lamb holding a cross with a flag attached to it.[194]

However, neither John Lawson nor John Hodgson maintained his role as a rich, successful businessman throughout his life. Several years earlier, Lawson had bought the shop in Cockerham, where he had served earlier as an apprentice under Henry Coward, but according to Stout, Lawson 'did not manage it to profit, through his misconduct, but about this time broke in a crazed condition'.[195] The worry of this and his involvement in the sugar house affected the elderly Lawson, and he died aged seventy-four in 1689. He was buried in the old Friends Burial Ground in Golgotha, Moorside, where a stone was erected over his grave. In 1951, this stone was removed to the Friends Meeting House in Lancaster, where it can be seen today at the side of the porch.

In his will, Lawson made no specific mention of the sugar house, but only an indirect reference to it involving a stable 'intended as a warehouse', presumably for the use of the refinery. However, two houses adjoining the stable were included in the will, one occupied by John's son-in-law James Myers, once the master of the ship the *Imployment*,

Lawson's token issued as the result of a shortage of small change.

Left: Lawson's gravestone in the Friends' Meeting House in Lancaster.

Below: Enlargement of the 1684 map to show the property mentioned in John Lawson's will.

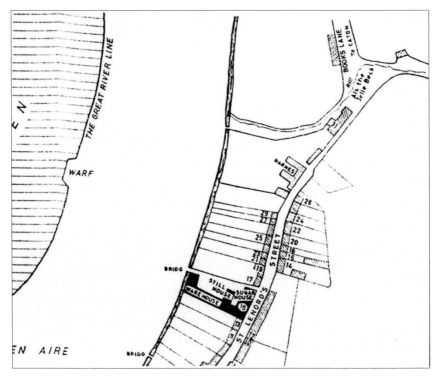

and the other by his son Robert. The houses' proximity to the sugar house suggests that the two men were involved in the administration of the refinery, and were possibly shareholders in a sugar house company that had been formed before John Lawson's death to include the younger members of the family.

Meanwhile according to Stout, John Hodgson 'met with losses, but continued to live high so that his credit began to decline and his debts in the customs to increase. Which when his wife, who was very high, perceived, it affected her so very much to be reduced, that she died, for grief as was supposed'.[196] Hodgson also became involved in a long legal wrangle concerning his dealings in tobacco. Eventually, the case was brought before the judges in London, and Hodgson, who owed a large sum in custom dues, was imprisoned as a debtor in Lancaster Castle, where he died in the early years of the eighteenth century.

Other members of the Lawson family continued to be involved in the establishment of Lancaster as an important port for the West Indian trade. In the early years of the eighteenth century, Robert Lawson and his brother Joshua established Sunderland Point as an outport for overseas cargoes bound for Lancaster. The channel of the Lune up to the town was difficult for sailing ships to navigate. In fact, some ships were 'brow-hauled' up the channel, while others had to offload their cargoes into lighters at the point. In the early years of the eighteenth century, a stone jetty was built at Sunderland Point to make it easier to unload cargoes across the sandy beach. Then, the brothers erected large warehouses on the leeward side of the peninsula, and later built a block maker's shop, an anchor smithy, and a rope walk.[197] In fact, the datestone for 1715 with Joshua Lawson's initials on it can still be seen on the warehouses that have now been converted into houses.

Joshua also built a house on the extreme point of the peninsula, where he could identify the ships as they approached the port with his merchandise – and get advanced warning to judge the state of the market. We could speculate that sugar might have been refined at Sunderland Point and re-exported without approaching the town of Lancaster, but we have no proof of that. Nevertheless, hogsheads of sugar would be unloaded there and reloaded into smaller vessels to sail up to the wharf in Lancaster.

The warehouses at Sunderland Point originally built to house cargoes destined for Lancaster, but now converted into houses.

Although no actual records remain concerning the operation of the sugar refinery in Lancaster in the early years of the eighteenth century, the fact that raw sugar was being imported through the port suggests that the refinery continued to operate under new management – possibly including the younger members of the Lawson family. Several contemporaries recorded the import of sugar through Lancaster. For instance in 1702, Stout reported that while the cotton from the wreck of the *Imployment* was sent to Manchester to be sold, the rescued sugar was auctioned in Lancaster, where the owners knew there was a ready market for it. John Langton of Kirkham also imported sugar into Lancaster in 1746 in the *Betty and* the *Martha* registered in Poulton.[198] In addition, there are also the testimonies of various visitors to the town, such as James Ray of Whitehaven, who reported in 1747 that Lancaster was a 'populous, thriving corporation' importing sugar from the West Indies, and John Crofts, a merchant from Bristol, who in 1759 also declared

The house at Sunderland Point built by Lawson.

that ships from Lancaster were importing sugar from the West Indies.[199]

The ready market for raw sugar in Lancaster was one of the reasons why Thomas Satterthwaite of Lancaster wrote in 1739 to his son Benjamin, who was in Barbados, asking him to send him sugar and rum, 'Which I can dispose of better than cotton.'[200] At that time, Benjamin was acting as a factor, or representative, for a group of Lancaster merchants that included members of the Townson, the Dilworth, and the Rawlinson families. Two years earlier at the age of nineteen, Benjamin had been an assistant in Barbados to another Quaker, twenty-seven-year-old Abraham Rawlinson. Abraham prospered in the West Indies and became one of the owners of the Goyave plantation on the island of Grenada, and also of the Fountain plantation on the island of St Vincent.[201] Later, he diversified and became involved in processing sugar at the refinery in Lancaster.

Despite the fact that many of the Quakers were successful merchants and leading townsmen, the established Church in Lancaster would not recognise the Quakers' objections to paying tithes. Both Robert Lawson and Abraham Rawlinson refused to contribute to that Church, and consequently their goods were distrained. The Quakers' book recording their 'sufferings' lists the amount taken from each of them; for instance, in 1749 Robert Lawson forfeited wheat and loaf sugar worth £1 17s 10d, while two years later he lost sugar and pewter worth £3 12s. Meanwhile, Abraham Rawlinson forfeited sugar worth £2 1s for his beliefs.

For sixty years, the sugar house continued in business, but little remains to record the details of its progress, that is until a glimpse is provided by the militia lists for Lancaster in 1757.[202] They included five militiamen with connections to the industry: Henry Hargreaves, who was listed among the partners in the sugar house during the 1760s, three sugar house men – Dennis and James Murphy, and Benjamin Moorby, and Richard Bailiff, described as the cooper at the sugar house. Whether this was the total labour force employed at the refinery at that time is unclear, but the fact that they were listed together suggests that they probably all lived within the complex. We have yet another glimpse of the organisation of the refinery by the fact that a cooper was fully employed at the sugar house complex. Evidently, he had a full time job repairing those huge hogsheads, which sometimes stood 6 feet tall, in preparation for their voyage back to the West Indies.

Another record of the elusive refinery appeared among the Chester documents,[203] as we have seen, when Joseph Manesty of Liverpool wrote to his partners in the Chester refinery in 1758 to tell them that Mr Marsden and the Lancaster sugar house were fulfilling orders from London for refined sugar. Presumably this was John Marsden, yet another Quaker, who had been 'a prentice to a friend' of the Lancaster Meeting. We can speculate that this friend was one of the Lawson family and that Marsden had been trained either as a sugar refiner or a sugar merchant. Certainly, he was in Lancaster for twenty years between 1742 and 1762, but according to the Quaker records, he then returned to Bristol.[204] What happened to him next is a mystery, but by 1768, Marsden – or his son – was in the north again, involved in the sale of the contents of the Lancaster sugar house – or were they the contents of the Chester sugar house?[205] That remains a mystery.

Meanwhile in the 1760s, Abraham Rawlinson had returned from the West Indies, and had become a partner in the refinery, which by that time had become the Lancaster Sugar House Company. The other five partners were Luke Astley, from Preston, who was made a freeman of Lancaster in 1747-48, Henry Hargreaves, Myles Birket, George Foxcroft, all from Lancaster, and significantly, Robert Lawson, thus confirming that the refinery's connection with the Lawson family had indeed continued. Although it is unclear exactly how long the six had been associated in the company, the continuing success of the partnership could be attributed to the fact that each brought his own expertise to the undertaking. Rawlinson had a vast experience of growing the cane, and his family owned several vessels that sailed on the West Indian route. Lawson and his family had years of experience in administering the sugar house in Lancaster. The Foxcroft family owned land adjacent to the sugar house. Myles Birket was a merchant based in Lancaster, who also had interests in iron furnaces in Leighton and Halton – a useful contact when heavy equipment was required.[206] He also had links with the West Indian trade through his son-in-law Dodshon Foster, who was one of the leading slave traders in Lancaster.[207] Henry Hargreaves was a skilled sugar refiner, married to Myles Birket's sister Elizabeth, while Luke Astley was a grocer based in Preston, who understood the final retailing of the product and had some experience as an importer and a shipowner.[208] It is also possible that he had family connections with Richard Astley, who was a partner in the Warrington refinery in the 1770s.

Although as usual, little is known of the employees of the sugar house, one foreign worker called Hartewick Griepenkerl is recorded in various documents. Whether he was German or Dutch is unclear, but he must have been a respected citizen of Lancaster, for he was made a freeman in 1748. The following year, he married Jane Fell of Urswick after a marriage bond had been issued on 28 July, naming John Singleton, another sugar baker and presumably one of his fellow workers, as bondsman.[209] Jane was a member of the Fell family of Swarthmoor Hall near Urswick, known for their connections with George Fox[210] and the birth of the Quaker movement, which as we have seen, was supported by many of the sugar refiners in Lancaster. Much later in the early nineteenth century, another foreign sugar worker was recorded as Joham Hinrich Holthusen.[211] The presence of these foreign workers among the labour force of the Lancaster sugar house is further evidence of an established pattern of immigration whereby foreign workers, particularly from Germany, worked in the sugar refineries of North West England.

By 1760, the sugar house company was so successful that the partners explored the possibility of expanding. At that time, the corporation of Lancaster was offering land for sale, so they applied and were successful in obtaining an area adjoining their property.[212] Six years later, they decided to expand still further, and this time Robert Foxcroft, the neighbouring landowner, granted them a lease of one year for land also adjoining the sugar house complex. They decided to buy that land, even though that meant finding still more capital. However, within the following year they had devised a way of buying it for £127. They divided the land into six lots and each of the partners bought one sixth on behalf of the company. This arrangement was entirely satisfactory until 1767, when Luke Astley died. However Robert Foxcroft, the original owner, agreed to take over his sixth share in the company. Two years later, there were more changes in the partnership, for Miles Birket and Robert Foxcroft wanted to withdraw. Their two, undivided sixth parts were shared between Robert Lawson, Abraham Rawlinson, and Henry Hargreaves, and a new lease was drawn up and witnessed by George Foxcroft.

The lease of 1769 gives us a detailed description of the lands that the company had acquired during the 1760s. It seems that the complex now extended from St Leonard's Gate back to the mill race of Lancaster mill, land on which there had formerly been an orchard and a barn. Within a year, the sugar house company had built a large building to be 'made use of as a sugar house for baking sugars and the offices, warehouses, and other buildings belonging thereto' on the orchard plot. The development also included a house and a brew house nearby. All these transactions in the 1760s are particularly interesting because they plot the spread of industry upstream on the banks of the River Lune, and thus date the urban expansion of Lancaster onto an area that was formerly rural.[213]

In 1768, the proposed sale of the sugar house at Lancaster was announced in the newspaper. However, this advertisement poses several problems. If the company had bought land to expand their operation, why had it decided to sell off their original premises? Was the company selling the old refinery now that it had built a more up-to-date one on Foxcroft's orchard? Unfortunately, the description gives no clue as to the age of the sugar house. Was the business yielding so much profit that the partners were content to share it with another company? Certainly, it would seem that they intended to sell the house as an

> ## To be SOLD,
> THE SUGAR HOUSE at LANCASTER, with three Pans, and all other Utensils necessary for carrying on the Work. The House stands distinct and separate from any other Buildings, has a spacious Yard belonging it, and the Buildings and Conveniencies are very good.
>
> For further Particulars apply to Henry Hargreaves who will be ready to shew the Premisses, and is authorised to treat for the same. 2-3n

The advertisement for the sale of the sugar house in 1768.

on-going concern, for the advertisement mentions the three pans and other utensils 'necessary for carrying on the work'. The refinery was described as an independent unit standing 'distinct and separate from any other buildings' – an advantage in view of the fire risk – and it had a 'spacious yard belonging to it'. All these factors would enable it to function separately. However, since the sale coincided with changes in the partnership, it is very possible that either the recent expansions had overstretched their finances, or it was a case of a new broom sweeping away the old ways and with them the old premises. Henry Hargreaves, the experienced sugar baker, was authorised to show anyone interested in the sale around the premises, and to negotiate with the potential buyer. An inventory was made, and it seems possible that eventually the contents of the sugar house were sold to Robert Hesketh of Chester, who was a partner in the Warrington refinery at that time.[214]

This last agreement suggests that Thomas Rawlinson had withdrawn from the sugar house when his brother died, leaving the business in the hands of the next generation of the Hargreaves family while he concentrated on his concerns as a merchant. In fact, an advertisement appeared in the *Preston Review* of 17 August 1793 instructing anyone who was interested in a sale that had been arranged for the disposal of a large amount of sugar to contact Thomas for the particulars. Interestingly, the advertisement made no mention of where to contact

> To be SOLD by AUCTION,
> At the MERCHANT's Coffee-Room, in
> LANCASTER,
> On TUESDAY the 20th of August, 1793,
> The SALE to begin at Ten o'Clock in the Forenoon,
> About 90 Hhds Granada fine Scale
> SUGAR,
> 40 Ditto St. Vincent ditto.
> Now landing out of the RAWLINSON,
> 143 Ditto Barbadoes ditto.
> 60 Barrels ditto.
> Now landing out of the BEST.
> For Particulars enquire of *Thomas Rawlinson,*
> *Efq;* Merchant; or *Wm. Sanderfon,* Broker.

Advertisement from the *Preston Review* for the sale of sugar. Enquirers are directed to Thomas Rawlinson, but no address is given as he was so well known in the town. (*Reproduced by kind permission of the Harris reference and Information Library, Preston*)

him; presumably, he was so well known that anyone in Lancaster would know where to find him. When Thomas died in 1803, he was described as a merchant, and by that time he had moved away from Lancaster and was living in Yealand, an attractive village several miles away.

Among the other merchants who had warehouses on Lancaster Quay in the 1780s, was John Addison, who was listed among the free burgesses of Lancaster in 1756. At that time, he was described as, 'Of Chester,' and his occupation was that of a sugar baker. He is not recorded as a sugar refiner elsewhere, so it is unclear whether he worked in Chester or Lancaster. However, it would seem that when he died in 1788, like Thomas Rawlinson he had retired from refining and was concentrating on his career as a merchant, with a warehouse and counting house in Lancaster. Again like the Rawlinson family, he also had an estate in the West Indies.[217]

The sugar refiner who took the Lancaster sugar house into the nineteenth century had links with the industry in Warrington, Liverpool, and Lancaster. He was George Crosfield, yet another Quaker, who had moved from Preston Patrick in Westmorland to Warrington in 1777 to be an assistant in Samuel Fothergill's grocery store. Eventually, he took over the shop, and in the course of his business, often went to Liverpool to order goods that were then conveyed back to Warrington by barge along the River Mersey.

The Crosfield family prospered in Warrington as this building, now part of the Unilever complex at Bank Quay, illustrates.

As a regular customer, he became known to the Liverpool merchants, and in 1799, two of them, Carson and Atherton, invited him to join them in a partnership to reopen the sugar refinery in Lancaster, which according to them, had been unoccupied for some time. Seemingly, when George Hargreaves died in 1794, it had been decided to close the sugar house. The previous ten years had been a time of deepening economic depression for Lancaster. The American War of Independence had disrupted trade, and two years of poor harvests in the plantations had affected Lancaster, leaving 2,214 people out of a population of 8,582 needing poor relief in 1783.[218] It was not the time to embark on a new partnership. George Hargreaves' brother James, who had been left a share in the sugar house in 1786, still lived in Springfield in Lancaster, but his business dealings had moved south and he claimed no interest whatsoever in the sugar house when he died in 1804. Instead, he had acquired a factory in Major Street in Manchester, which he left to James

Grierson, possibly a fustian manufacturer.[219] He also stated that he was in partnership with his cousin Henry Hargreaves of New Church in Rossendale, to whom he bequeathed all his possessions in the West Indies.[220]

Despite the fact that he was faced with the difficult task of reopening the abandoned sugar house, George Crosfield was very enthusiastic about both his move to Lancaster and his appointment as the manager, and he started work in October 1799. Two years later, disaster struck and the refinery was burned to the ground. Crosfield recorded in his diary on 9 October 1801, 'Memorable for an event that was truly awful and alarming to us all, which was the sugar house being burnt to the ground.'[221] Undeterred, Crosfield ensured that by the following January it was completely rebuilt, and work was resumed. However the refinery, in common with many of the industries in Lancaster, experienced great difficulties during the Napoleonic Wars. The French threat to the British ships trading with the West Indies was so great that in 1798, the government decided that the only way to counter the danger was to make it compulsory to sail in convoys. Since those convoys operated from Liverpool, most of the Lancaster merchants and their ships moved south, and a year later, even the slave merchants were compelled by law to move to Liverpool. Imports from the West Indies through the port of Lancaster fell from 11,562 tons in 1799 to 1,668 tons in 1802.[222]

Although his two partners Carson and Atherton left the business in July 1809, Crosfield struggled alone to keep the business operating. In the hope of some improvement after the war, he entered into another partnership, this time with Thomas Giles.[223] However, when the war ended in 1815, too many difficulties confronted them. The West Indian island of St Croix, which was one of the main sources of Lancaster's sugar, was ceded to Denmark by the Treaty of Vienna. The larger ships that carried the raw sugar across the Atlantic did not return to Lancaster, as they needed deeper water and the port was rapidly silting up. Then there was the fact that the machinery in the refinery was outdated, and more investment was needed to modernise the plant and install the new vacuum process. It was hopeless to continue refining sugar under those conditions, so finally George decided to move back into the wholesale grocery business. Sugar refining in Lancaster was abandoned for a second time.

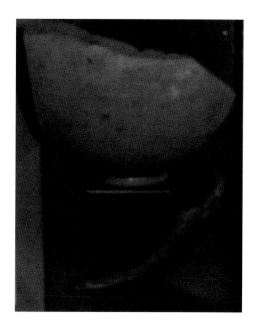

The sugar moulds in the Lancaster Maritime Museum.

When the foundations of the Cooperative Garage – now Curry's store on the industrial estate – were being excavated in 1929, archaeologists investigated the sugar house site in Phoenix Street off St Leonardsgate. They found several pieces of red terracotta pottery sugar moulds, which are now in the Maritime Museum at St George's Quay. It is possible that this was the site of a pottery that manufactured sugar moulds for the old refinery. However, excavations on the site of Mitchell's brewery also produced sugar moulds. Further research would be needed to ascertain whether this was the site of another pottery or possibly of a nineteenth century sugar house. Although moulds have been found near St Patrick's Chapel at Heysham, it is more likely that they were part of a cargo heading towards the West Indies that never reached its destination.

Whitehaven

Whitehaven's sugar refining industry was established for reasons that were quite different from those affecting the other towns in this study. Whereas the industry in those towns grew as a response to outside forces, particularly to the ability to import the raw material from the

West Indies, sugar refining was established in Whitehaven as a response to the need for a market for a local resource, the abundance of coal in the area. Although coal was available for the industry in the southern towns, it had to be brought some distance to the ports. In Whitehaven, the coal was on the coast, and the need to find an additional outlet for the local stocks was one of the primary reasons for the foundation of its sugar industry.

Sir Christopher Lowther was the first to realise the potential of Whitehaven as a centre for the exploitation of the vast coal seams of the Cumbrian coast. When he inherited the estate in the early seventeenth century, Whitehaven was only a small fishing village lying along the Pow Beck beneath the Kell's headland. Nevertheless, he could envisage its development into a port to export the coal that lay in rich seams beneath his property. In 1634, he built a small pier to encourage larger ships to use the harbour, which had the advantage of having mines in the immediate vicinity. The proximity of Whitehaven to the Irish coast was yet another of the town's advantages, because it was a much shorter voyage across the Irish Sea to supply the demand for coal in Ireland than it was from the ports in south Lancashire.

When Sir Christopher died in 1644, his estate passed to his son Sir John Lowther, who expanded the port and developed the fishing village of about 250 inhabitants into a model Georgian town of over 2,000 townsfolk. Upon gaining control, his first priority was to secure the economy of the villagers by obtaining the right of the town to hold a weekly market and fair. Then he concentrated on encouraging ship building and improving the harbour facilities. Land transport for heavy goods was extremely difficult, especially across the Lakeland countryside that formed the hinterland of the town. Packhorses could only carry a limited weight, and wagons could not travel along muddy, hilly tracks. Consequently, most heavy goods were transported by sea around the coast from Whitehaven to other British ports. Therefore, if a product was to be sold in any quantity beyond the immediate area, good harbours and ships were essential. That applied particularly to the export of coal, and later to sugar.

As well as improving the harbour, Sir John extended the village and divided the land intended for his new town into a rectangular grid of roads, with blocks of land between them divided into plots 15 feet wide. These he leased to tenants, who could build anything they wanted upon them – houses, shops, workshops, or warehouses – so long as they conformed to his strict grid system. It has been suggested that his ideas on town planning originated from 'a possible relationship with Sir Christopher Wren',[224] but whether that is true or not, his plans certainly accommodated the development of buildings for industrial purposes.

Meanwhile, more ships were using the little harbour for the redistribution of goods by coastal trade. One of the earliest references to the import of sugar through Whitehaven comes from a case heard at the Court of the Exchequer in 1687, when 'the great traders' Addison and Inman of Carlisle were described as importing sugar and molasses through the port.[225] Although these products came to the port, there were no facilities for refining them, and so they would be re-exported to the southern ports in coastal vessels and delivered to the established refineries at Liverpool and Chester. Other products that were redistributed in this way included rice from the East, tobacco from Virginia, wines and prunes from the Mediterranean, cod fish and oil from Newfoundland, timber from Norway, and flax and tar from the Baltic.[226]

By the 1690s, the new township of Whitehaven was firmly established, and Sir John Lowther was planning to develop a sugar refining industry alongside the harbour to utilise his great natural resource of coal. In fact, we have a letter sent to him by John Gale from Whitehaven on 17 April 1698 mentioning the fact when he objects to the imposition of taxes on coal. He wrote, 'Sir, We are here much alarmed with the imposition upon coals (as appears in the votes), the common sentiments rather inclining to chimney money as a far more equal tax...' Then, he explained that hundreds of pounds had already been spent in building an iron works, a copper works, and a pottery in the town to take advantage of the cheap coal. These were 'all at a stand', and no-one [would] proceed further with the projects, for if the price of coal was increased by taxation, there would be no profit to be made in those industries. Almost as an afterthought he added, 'I might further add to these a glass house, and a sugar house, both which will be suppressed.'[227] Of course, this does not mean that either the sugar house or the glasshouse was already in existence, but certainly there were plans to introduce them as new industries to the town. The proposed tax on coal threatened the completion of those projects.

The next member of the Lowther family to promote the development of the town was Sir James Lowther, and by 1712, the sugar house had been built at the harbour end of Duke Street at the corner with Strand Street. [228] The next task was to find someone to manage it, and so Sir James enlisted the help of William Gilpin, his agent in Whitehaven. Evidently, he had already approached the agent's brother with an offer of the post of manager, for in a letter written from London on 29 November 1712, he complained to the agent that his brother had not given him a firm answer to the proposition that he should manage the new sugar house. [229] Meanwhile, Sir James had found a merchant in Whitehaven who was willing to cooperate in the venture. A tentative arrangement was made that this merchant would provide the stock of sugar, and in return he would receive half of the profit made from the refining. Sir James – or his advisers – had worked out how much stock would be needed and how much profit could be made, taking into account that they would be able to use coal from the local pits to heat the boilers, and so reduce the usual costs. Sir James sent these figures to the agent to pass on to his brother in the hope of convincing William that there would be 'little hazard' or risk for him in the project, and so persuading him to agree.

Despite the favourable accounts, the agent's brother was not convinced, and replied that he felt it would be too great an undertaking. However, Sir James did not accept this as his final answer, and continued trying to persuade him, assuring him in yet another letter of 14 December 1712 that, 'Those that will engage in it may make it as small as they please and have the security in their own hands.' [230] In other words, he was prepared to allow the manager himself to dictate how small or how ambitious the project should be, and so he would be able to control the amount of risk involved. Sir James could not conceal his enthusiasm for the venture – and for the profit it would yield. He reported that when he was in London, he had heard reports of the huge profits gained by entrepreneurs who had invested in sugar refineries. He was convinced that 'the profit [would] be great in proportion' if the sugar sold as it did in London. He added a further inducement that the sugar would be sold for ready money. Consequently, the refiner would not have to wait for payment, as was the case in so many undertakings at that time.

Although he still did not succeed in persuading Gilpin, Sir James refused to abandon the project, and in the following month, sent a letter to his agent suggesting that a Mr Barwise would make a good manager and might accept the position if it was offered to him.[231] Although Mr Barwise does not seem to have had had any experience in refining sugar, he did have the distinct advantage of being related to Mr Humphrey Senhouse, who was the local agent for the sale and distribution of West Indian sugar. Incidentally, the day book in which Mr Senhouse recorded many of his transactions has been preserved for us. His entry for June 1704 is interesting, for it recorded that he had sold 4 cwt of sugar and had distributed the profit to various relatives and others who had invested in the cargo.[232] As we have seen, similar transactions were made during the early development of Liverpool's sugar trade, as when William Blundell distributed the profits made from the *Antelope*'s voyage to the West Indies to his relatives who had invested in the project. It would seem that the financial support of relatives was important if these early ventures were to succeed.

Mr Senhouse's prominence in the Whitehaven sugar trade suggests that he was probably the anonymous local merchant who had agreed tentatively to supply sugar to the proposed sugar house. Certainly, Sir James was anxious not to offend him, for he advised Gilpin, 'Mention it first to Mr Humphrey Senhouse ... He will take it well to have the first offer, and if [Barwise] declines, [Senhouse] will be more ready to engage another.' Evidently, the whole situation required diplomatic handling, and consequently, Sir James insisted that Humphrey Senhouse had to be consulted even though he thought 'he will not be concerned, as living at a distance.'

Mr Barwise seemed an ideal candidate for the post, as he was already an established resident in Whitehaven, having rented a tenement, No. 39 Queen Street, for 5s a week since 1709. Again, Sir James stressed the point that 'the profit is great for one that will have an eye over it and deliver in and take out the sugars after they are refined so that they will have the security in their own hands.' Evidently, it was still very doubtful whether Barwise would accept the position, for Sir James concluded by saying, 'I wish you could think of somebody that will be content to play at small gain and be concerned in refining small parcels to be sold for ready money in the town and neighbourhood.' However, none of these difficulties deterred Sir James, who still retained his enthusiasm for the project, assuring his agent, 'Very great works of this sort arise from contemptible beginnings.' Perhaps that forecast influenced Mr Barwise, for he accepted the post and continued as manager of the sugar house until the late 1720s.

The sugar house was so successful under Barwise that he decided to extend his interests and move from Whitehaven to Workington in 1726 to set up another sugar house. Seemingly, according to a report from the customs officers in 1727,[233] he was then in partnership with James Milham, a Virginia merchant. Of course, Sir James was well aware of the new developments, and confirmed his satisfaction with Barwise's decision in a letter to John Spedding, his agent in Whitehaven. He wrote from London on 30 April 1726, 'Mr Curwin tells me Barwise is going to set up a sugar house at Workington. That a nailery is also going forward, these both which I was mightily pleased with.'[234] However, that was not the end of Barwise's ambitions, for by the following year, according to the customs officers' reports, he was managing a distillery in Workington as well as the two sugar houses. Seemingly, new industries were being established very rapidly at this time in the towns on the west Cumbrian coast as a result of the availability of the cheap coal on the Lowther estates.

Unfortunately Mr. Barwise's success was short lived, as Sir James learnt from this letter sent by John Spedding on 21 April 1728: 'Sir, You were very fortunate in getting your money off Barwise the sugar boiler who is now under arrest for about £180, which with other things that he owes amount to about £450, so if his creditors are not willing to compound he will consent to a commission of bankruptcy.'[235] Unfortunately, we have no details of this case except for the fact that Barwise's ambitions had caused him to extend his commitments too far and too quickly. Again, we find a parallel in a similar situation in Chester, when Joseph Manesty speculated too heavily on the future of the sugar trade and was made bankrupt. By contrast, the fortunes of the Lowther family were soaring. Robert, who had been posted to Barbados as governor in 1704 as a relatively poor man, invested in the sugar plantations, and as he was able to supervise the administration of his own plantations, his profits rose to £30,466 during the twenty-three years from 1722 to 1745.[236] He returned to Whitehaven a very rich man, no doubt owing much of his success to the infamous slave trade.

After Barwise's bankruptcy, the sugar refinery in Whitehaven was taken over by William Gilpin, who was the son of the former agent, in partnership with his brother (or possibly his uncle) John Gilpin. We

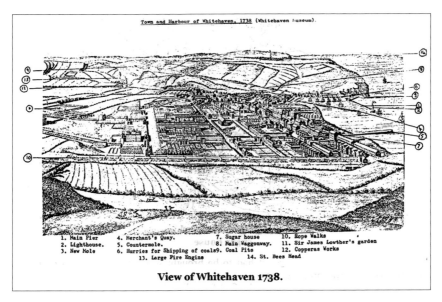

View of Whitehaven 1738.

know little about its management at this time except that two ships with sugar for William Gilpin & Co. entered Whitehaven harbour, one in 1739 and another in 1741.[237] If the whole cargo of sugar was bound for the refinery at Whitehaven, the capacity of the refinery must have been increased considerably, for as we have seen, the original plant was intended to refine only 'small parcels' of sugar. The support of the Senhouse family continued at least until 1737, when it was reported that they got their supplies of sugar from the sugar house in Whitehaven.[238]

Sugar continued to arrive in the port on the *Mermaid* from Antigua on 26 July 1743, certainly destined for the local sugar company.[239] Then in 1753, the slaver *Providence* returned to Whitehaven with forty-one hogsheads and twelve tierces of sugar.[240] Whether this cargo was also destined for the sugar house is not stated. However, we know that the refinery was certainly still in existence, for sometime between 1753 and 1755, Angerstein, the traveller from Sweden, visited the town and recorded in his diary that sugar loaves were made in the town, and that the master refiner came from Hamburg, another instance of a craftsman from the continent working in the industry. He noted that the customs duty inflated the price of sugar in Whitehaven, where it was 12*d* per pound, while it was only 9½*d* in Hamburg.[241]

This put the British refiners at a great disadvantage, for they had to pay 4s and 9d in custom dues on each hundredweight of raw sugar. The sugar boilers nationwide decided to combine and to send a petition complaining about the high price of the raw sugar when it was imported into England. In fact, Whitehaven was included among the 129 places mentioned in a petition to Parliament in 1753.[242] Although the petition stated that the typical number of workers employed in a refinery was six members of the family and nine hired workers,[243] it is unlikely that the Whitehaven sugar house would have employed so many. The number quoted in the petition was an average from all the refineries in the country, and perhaps would not be typical of the one in the remote North West.

Despite these difficulties, Whitehaven sugar house did continue in business, if only on a comparatively small scale. This meant that there was only a limited demand for raw sugar at the port. As there was no competition between agents to purchase the sugar in Whitehaven – unlike there was in Liverpool – the refinery had the final control over the price it would pay the importer for the raw sugar. That may have been an advantage for the refiners, but it did not encourage the merchants or the sea captains to sell their cargoes of sugar in Whitehaven.

In fact, the next news we have of the sugar house is an advertisement for its sale in the *Cumberland Pacquet* on 10 November 1774. As it was the only refinery in Whitehaven, the agents thought a description was unnecessary, so unfortunately we are given very few details of the property except that there was a warehouse adjoining it. The only reason for the sale seems to be that the refinery was not buying enough raw sugar to induce the captains to bring their cargoes for sale in Whitehaven. If the supply of raw sugar was limited, the profit for the owners would also be limited. Indeed, William Senhouse, who was in Barbados supervising his sugar plantation, wrote a letter to his brother Humphrey in 1787, which confirms that this was the case. He wrote:

> I have sent this year 10,000 or 11,000 lb of fine cotton ... to be sold at Liverpool ... We made too between twenty or thirty hogsheads of excellent sugar besides rum so that this year we have done tolerably well and the prospects of the next is now better ... Have long wished for a Maryport or Whitehaven ship to call.[244]

SUGAR HOUSE

Whitehaven, November 10, 1774.

TO BE SOLD in Public Sale (this Evening) at Mr HAILE's Coffee Room, the SUGAR-HOUSE in this town; with all the Water houses adjoining, and other Accomodations.

An advertisement for the sale of the sugar house in 1774.

If the ships did not bring the raw sugar into Whitehaven, the refinery simply could not function.

However, sugar refining on a small scale did continue in Whitehaven into the nineteenth century, for according to contemporary directories, the sugar house was run by Johnson and Manley in the early 1820s, and in 1829 by Edward Johnson & Co.[245] What happened after the sale in 1774 until the 1820s is unclear, but certainly Johnson and Manley were not refiners in 1811, but were described as grocers in the directory. They must have expanded into sugar refining later, and by the 1830s, the sugar house complex was a considerable size. It had extended along Catherine Street, and appears on J. R. Wood's map of Whitehaven. Of course, it is difficult to ascertain how much of the site was actually the sugar refinery or whether it included various ancillary industries.

It seems very likely that by this time, the refinery was acting in conjunction with Whitehaven's distillery to produce the molasses essential for that industry. The Jefferson family had established a rum distillery in Lowther Street in the early 1780s, and in 1785, produced the first known brand of rum distilled in England, Jefferson's Rum. The custom of making rum butter and eating it at christenings and other celebrations in Cumbria may have been developed as a result of the success of Whitehaven's distillery. Certainly, that industry continued to be very successful under the guidance of six generations of the family, and only closed in the 1970s, before being converted into a tourist attraction for the twenty-first century.[246]

Although during the 1720s it seemed as though sugar refining on the

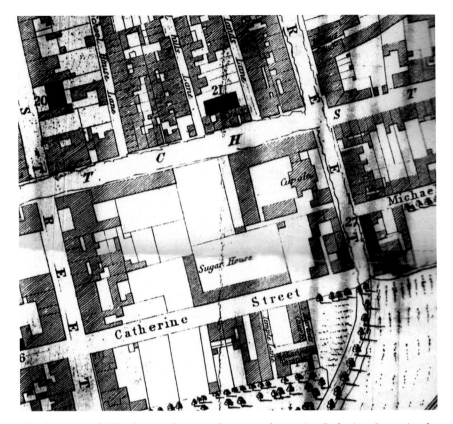

Wood's map of Whitehaven showing the sugar house in Catherine Street in the nineteenth century.

Cumbrian coast would expand into a sizeable industry, that was not to be, and all Sir James' dreams of 'very great works' came to nought. The position of Whitehaven, which had been originally a great advantage when the transport of heavy goods relied mainly upon the sea, proved to be a disadvantage once canals and turnpike roads were constructed across south Lancashire. Then it was no problem to take the coal to fuel the boilers by canal to Liverpool, and to distribute the refined sugar to all the large centres of the population that had developed in that area. The port facilities in Liverpool were being improved constantly to cater for even larger ships, and the market in the city for imported sugar was flourishing. Consequently, sugar refining concentrated in that port and was finally abandoned in the lesser ports such as Whitehaven.

CHAPTER 6

Conclusion

This investigation has answered many of the questions that had intrigued me when I embarked on this study, but in doing so, has also revealed more problems that cannot be solved until more documentary sources become available. My quest for reasons as to why the industry was originally established in the North West has provided different motives for each location. Of course, the simplistic answer always has been that the ports were easily accessible for ships coming from the West Indies. That is true, but without the improvements in the docks and quays that were undertaken by Liverpool Town Council, by Lord Lowther in Whitehaven, and by John Lawson in Lancaster, those ports would have been unable to handle a volume of shipping sufficient enough to make the industry viable. Similarly, raw sugar could not have been transported in the quantity needed to make refining in Warrington and Manchester worthwhile without the merchants of Warrington and Manchester making the Mersey navigable and constructing the Mersey and Irwell Navigation.

Once a port had been found that could handle the imported raw sugar, the next problem was the accessibility of the raw materials required by the industry. Fuel for the boilers was most important, and one of the advantages for the development of the industry in Warrington, Manchester, and Whitehaven was that coal was readily available from the coalfields nearby. Liverpool had a history of exporting coal to Ireland, so there was no problem in transporting coal to that town, while Lancaster and Chester were already well served by coastal vessels that brought coal to the towns from North Wales or South Lancashire. Water was also needed in vast quantities, and the North West had no difficulty in supplying that from its many existing wells, plus of course, more wells could be dug when they were needed. Manpower was the final ingredient, and that too was readily available. The population of the whole area rapidly expanded once the plague had been conquered and the carnage and deprivation of the Civil War were over.

The expanding population in the North West and its gradually increasing wealth produced an ever-increasing local demand for sugar. Until the mid-seventeenth century, sugar had been regarded as a luxury to be given to visitors or to be eaten at celebrations. However, once the cane fields in the British West Indies had been established, the price of raw sugar was reduced and more people could afford to buy refined sugar. This demand was increased when the Government imposed lighter taxes on colonial sugar, thus making it cheaper and so within the consumer's budget. The industry could not have succeeded without that demand.

Similarly, without the entrepreneurs – most of them from among the ranks of the merchants – there could have been no industry. Their trading interests had expanded with the establishment of the transatlantic trade, first into tobacco plantations in North America and then into the sugar cane fields in the West Indies. They had plenty of wealth to invest, and so in order to guarantee an ever-increasing demand for their cargoes, they built more refineries and established more companies. The need to find an industry to use the coal from his coal field made Lord Lowther venture into sugar refining in Whitehaven, while the demand for molasses for distilling prompted John Hodgson and John Lawson to establish the Lancaster refinery.

Although many of the later refiners were local residents, other factors brought the early pioneers to the North. The plague and the fire that closed the port of London and destroyed its facilities were the 'push' factors that made Smith and Danvers move to Liverpool and establish the town's first refinery. Henthorne also came to Chester from London, and his close connections with merchants dealing in sugar in Antwerp, Amsterdam, and London influenced his decision to invest in refining. The success of the early pioneers convinced the next generation that investment in the sugar refining industry would prove very profitable.

Unfortunately there are no reliable statistics to use for charting the increasing production of the refineries. The mid-eighteenth century was definitely a time of increased activity in the industry, but undoubtedly, our perception of the amount of that increase is coloured by the greater availability of information for that time. New partnerships were formed, and although that could be a sign of success, several resulted from the deaths of the original partners. Many new refineries were built at this time, for instance in Lancaster and Warrington, but although it is obvious that this expansion was prompted by an increasing demand for sugar, it is impossible to quantify the output of the industry.

The decline of the industry in some parts of the region is easier to assess. The fate of the industry in both Lancaster and Chester was dependent on their rivers. The estuaries of the Lune and the Dee silted up rapidly, which prevented the more modern, larger ships from docking near the refineries. The barrels had to be transferred into barges for the short journey up the rivers. These difficulties caused the industry to contract, until finally the Lancaster refinery had to close, and the Roberts family were the only refiners left to maintain production on the banks of the Dee. The docks in Whitehaven were close to the refinery, but here, unlike the position in southern Lancashire, the demand from the immediate hinterland was very small. The population in the Lake District was not expanding, and transporting heavy goods over the fells was difficult. Sugar refined in Whitehaven had to be distributed further away from the town by sea, and that added to the cost. Distilling produced a more valuable product, and consequently, sugar refining in Whitehaven became a part of the production of rum, both for the Navy and for the local inhabitants' traditional treat of rum butter.

Ormskirk, Preston, and North Meols refineries represented short-lived attempts by local entrepreneurs to take part in the success of the industry. In the case of Ormskirk, it was greed that destroyed the project, and as far as Preston and North Meols are concerned, we know so little about them that it is impossible to analyse their demise. Manchester and Warrington refineries on the other hand survived much longer, despite the challenge of the booming cotton and metal working industries. A new refinery opened in Chester Street in Manchester, but it could not compete with the Warrington refinery, which moved to the banks of the Sankey Canal. Sankey sugar survived and was sold nationwide during the next two centuries.

The refineries in Liverpool achieved their great success in our period because of the upgrading of the dock facilities in Liverpool, which assured that port of success. They also avoided most of the difficulties encountered by their rivals. Nevertheless, those early refineries in various parts of the North West were the foundations on which Liverpool's resounding success as the capital of the British sugar industry in the nineteenth and twentieth centuries was built.

This study has revealed many of the reasons for the development and failure of the various sugar refineries in the North West, and also it has painted a wider picture of the gradual disappearance of the rural aspect of the towns as industry spread into the area. In the later years, pigs and hens no longer featured in the inventories of the sugar refiners, and the fields that appeared in close proximity to the sugar houses in Liverpool and other towns had been replaced by houses and industrial buildings on the later maps.

Another unexpected outcome that has been revealed is the amount of interaction between the refiners, and also the mobility of the workforce. They were not units who worked in isolation, but continually communicated with each other checking the state of the trade in the various areas. Although there is little evidence about the actual workers; the Ormskirk example illustrates the fact that they knew of opportunities to work in other refineries, and as a result were not averse to moving to other towns if necessary.

Beneath all this interaction there were often religious bonds, which may have cemented the cooperation between the refiners in the different areas. There may even be connections with the Rowntree foundation of today through the links with Quakerism. An investigation into that aspect of the establishment of the industry would form an interesting study for the future.

Notes

Chapter 1: Introducing the Sugar Industry

1. J. A. C. Hugill ed., *Sugar* (Cosmo Pubications: 1949) First published 1936, p. 24

2. L. A. G. Strong, *The Story of Sugar* (George Weidenfeld & Nicolson: 1954) p. 87. This book presents an excellent overview of the production and uses of sugar, concentrating particularly on the nineteenth century.

3. Charles Wilson, *England's Apprentice Ship 1603-1763* (Longmans, Green & Co.: 1965) p. 286

4. For further information see: J. H. Galloway, *The Sugar Cane Industry* (CambridgeUniversity Press: 1989); Richard Dunn, *Sugar and Slaves, the Rise of the planter class in the English West Indies, 1624-1713* (Virginia University Press: 1972); L. A. G. Strong, *The Story of Sugar* (Weidenfeld & Nicolson: 1954); Arthur Mee ed., *Harmsworth Self-Educator*, vol.5 1906 (Carmelite House: 1906) p. 3,653

5. Dorothy Davies, *A History of Shopping* (Routledge and Kegan Paul: 1966) p. 93

6. J. A. C. Hugill ed., *Sugar* (Cosmo Publications: 1949) p. 7

7. Dunn, *Sugar and Slaves* p. 41

8. Lancashire Record Office (later referred to as LRO). WCW Robert Jump of North Meols 1614

9. Strong, *The Story of Sugar* p. 80-83; Mee, *Self Educator*, p. 3,653

10. Sidney W. Mintz, *Sweetness and Power. The Place of Sugar in Modern*

History (Viking: 1985) p. 37

11. Noel Deer, *The History of Sugar* (Chapman & Hall: 1949), p. 458

12. Sidney W. Mintz, *Sweetness and Power*, p. 37

13. J. A. Twemlow ed., *Liverpool Town Books vol. II* (Liverpool University Press: 1935) p. 240

14. Davies, *A History of Shopping* p. 93

15. Liverpool Town Book 17 November 1648, in G. Chandler, *Liverpool Under Charles I* (Liverpool Libraries: 1957) p. 382

16. Elizabeth French (transcriber), *List of Emigrants to America from Liverpool 1697-1707* (Baltimore Genealogical Publishing Co. Inc.: 1983) p. 25

17. The reports of the agents from the islands to the Council of Trade and Plantations in England are recorded in the Calendar of State Papers for America and the West Indies. Q325-342, Rec.3032, p. 10, p. 668

18. Gomer Williams, *History of the Liverpool Privateers with an Account of the Liverpool Slave Trade* (Heinemann: 1897)

19. The obituary of Richard Maudsley in *The Mary Borough Chronicle* 30 January 1920, which also recorded several of his other experiences as a sugar grower

20. *The Queenslander* of 5 September 1935

21. Robert F. Osborn, *Valiant Harvest. The Founding of the South African Sugar Industry 1848-1926* (South African Sugar Association: 1964)

22. R. R. Angerstein, *Illustrated Travel Diary 1753-1755 Industry in England and Wales from a Swedish Perspective* (Science Museum: 2001) p. 304

23. A. C. Barnes, *The Sugar Cane* (2nd edition, Leonard Hill Books: 1974) p. 6-7, see also *Journal of the Merseyside Archaeological Society Vol 5* 1982-83, p. 64

24. John Gore, 'Directory for 1895' reproduced in *An Everyday History of Liverpool* (Scouse Press. ND) unpaged.

25. C. Foster, *Cheshire Cheese* THSLC vol. 144 (1995), p. 18

26. J. J. Bagley, *A History of Lancashire* (sixth edition, Phillimore: 1976) p. 78

27. *Ibid.* p. 80

28. Liverpool R.O.: Parish register for St Nicholas' Church, Liverpool 6 February 1666

29. Liverpool R.O.: Liverpool Port Books, E190/1337/16 pp. 21-22. I am indebted to Jo McCann for drawing my attention to this information

30. C. Northcote Parkinson suggested in his book *The Rise of the Port of Liverpool* (Liverpool University Press: 1952) p. 54, that Blundell bought the linen illicitly from Ireland, but that seems unlikely, because flax was processed, 'retted', in the Ormskirk area and linen was sold in the local market at that time. As a recusant, Blundell would have hesitated to be involved in illegal trading with Ireland

31. A butt contained a larger amount of sugar than a hogshead

32. Margaret Blundell, ed. *Cavalier, Letters of William Blundell to his Friends 1620-1698* (Longmans Green: 1933) p. 119

33. Bagley, *A History of Lancashire*, p. 80

34. Charles Wilson, *England's Apprenticeship 1603-1763* (Longmans Green: 1965) p. 169

35. Hugh Cunliffe, *The Story of Sunderland Point* (Author: 1994) p. 6

36. J. D. Marshall ed. et al, *The Autobiography of William Stout of Lancaster 1665-1752*, (MUP), pp. 138-140. (Marshall, 1851) p. 62-3

37. Cunliffe, *The Story of Sunderland Point*, p. 13

38. Captain William Hutchinson was dock master and water bailiff for Liverpool 1759-1793. He established Britain's first lifeboat station at Formby in 1770s

39. LRO WCW James Berry of Ormskirk 1686

40. Strong, *The Story of Sugar*, p. 85

41. See chapter on Liverpool sugar refineries

42. For further information on the triangular trade see: M. Elder, *The Slave Trade and the Economic Development of Eighteenth Century Lancaster* (Ryburn: 1992)

Chapter 2: The Liverpool Refineries

43. 'The Moore Rental', Thomas Heywood ed. CS 1847, Vol. 12. (folio 71v), pp. 76-78

44. *Diary of Samuel Pepys* for 2nd September 1666 (Henry Bohn: 1858) Vol. 2, p. 441

45. *Ibid.*, 6 September 1666, p. 448

46. J. J. Bagley, *The History of Lancashire* (Phillimore: 1976) p. 81

47. E. W. Gilboy, *Wages in 18th Century England* (Harvard: 1934) p. 220

48. Heywood, ed. *The Moore Rental*, pp. 76-78

49. Tyndale Harries W., *Landmarks in Liverpool History* (Philip Son & Nephew: 1961) p. 37

50. Daniel who married Susan Smith, was the second son of Anthony Danvers of Horley Manor in Oxford. The family later sold the manor and moved to Holborn in London. LRO E. J. Danvers, 'Danvers of the City of Liverpool in the Seventeenth and Eighteenth Century; an extension of the work of F. M. Manamara in his 'Memorials of the Danvers Family', unpaged, ND

51. CRO EDC 51687 No.37 Liverpool. This was typical of the behaviour of many of the non-conformists at that time. The dissenters attended their own services, often led by ministers who had been ejected from the established Church following the Act of Uniformity of 1662, and so did not attend their parish churches

52. PRO C134/W & M 1692

53. H. Peet, *Liverpool in the reign of Queen Anne* (Henry Young & Sons: 1908) p. 43, p. 101

54. LRO WCW Samuel Danvers, merchant of Liverpool 1719/20

55. Formerly Isabel Crooke of Abram

56. Similarly in Ormskirk a wealthy tanner, Thomas Brandreth built his large house next to his tan pits, which must have smelt abominably.

57. George Chandler, *Liverpool* (Batsford: 1957) p. 332

58. LRO WCW Isaac Oldham 1782

59. LRO WCW William Skelhorne 1789. Skelhorne's wife's maiden name was Greves and a John Hermann Greves died in 1770. It is possible that he was her father. in law of William Skelhorne. The name suggests a link with the immigrant German sugar workers

60. 'The Norris Papers' 5 January 1702(3), Thomas Heywood ed. CS vol. 9, OS 1846, p. 116

61. J. A. Picton, *Memorials of Liverpool*, (Gilbert G. Walmesley: 1903) Vol. 1, p. 179

62. Enfield W., *An Essay Towards the History of Liverpool*, 1773 Facsimile (Rondo Publications: 1972)

63. J. J. Bagley, *A History of Lancashire*, p. 81

64. Bruce Lenman, *The Jacobite Risings in Britain 1689-1746* (Eyre

Metheun Ltd.: 1980) p. 158; Rupert C. Jarvis, *Collected Papers on the Jacobite Risings*, (MUP: 1972), Vol.2, p. 264; Don Higham, *Liverpool and the '45 Rebellion* (Countyvise: 1995) p. 109-110

65. Cumbria Record Office at Kendal. WD/AG1/8

66. A plan of Liverpool and the Pool 1650 copied from the original drawing in the Court of the Duchy of Lancaster. *A Portfolio of Maps* (Scouse Press)

67. Matthew Street appears on a lease in 1738, when Joseph Stanley consolidated his holding in the area. It has been claimed that this street was named after a slave trader, but my research suggests that it was named after a Liverpool landowner

68. Also described as an ironmonger from Temple Bar in the 1766 directory

69. The earliest precautions taken by the council in July 1650 were to buy 'twelve leather buckets and 4 or 6 hooks made for pulling down any house on fire, which God defend'. Michael Power ed., 'Liverpool Town Books 1649-1671' (RSLC) Vol. 136, 1998, p. 9

70. Henry Peet, ed., *Liverpool Vestry Books 1681-1834* (Liverpool University Press: 1912) folio 146 v, p. 165, Castle Hey was an alternative name for Harrington St

71. LRO WCW Richard Cribb April 1755. He mentions his house in Duke Street, which at that time led into open farm land.

72. Kendal R. O. WD/AG1/8, 19

73. The name acknowledged that Peter Rainford was the early developer of the site

74. Unfortunately that document has been lost

75. CRO Hincks Papers H/59. See also in the chapter on the Chester refinery

76. LRO WCW John Bridge of Liverpool, 1763

77. An earlier James Laithwaite appears in the records of the Ormskirk refinery in the 1680s, but it is impossible to draw any connection with this tenant without further documentary evidence

78. LRO WCW Henry Rauthmell 1787

79. LRO WCW James Gildart of Whiston 1790

80. LRO WCW William Farrer of Preston 1795

81. LRO WCW John Baicklin of Liverpool 1781

82. Stephen Waterworth lived at 76 Dale Street. (1790 Lewis's directory)

83. H. Peet, *Liverpool in the Reign of Queen Anne* (Henry Young & Sons: 1908) p. 40, p. 108

84. LRO WCW John Knight merchant of Liverpool 1774

85. Wardle and Bentham's Commercial Directory for 1814

86. In his book *Liverpool: A People's History* (Carnegie: 1993) Peter Aughton claimed that Daniel Danvers owned one of these refineries in Harrington Street prior to 1708, but I have been unable to corroborate that

87. George Chandler, *Liverpool* (Batsford: 1957) p. 332

88. A. C. Cumming, *Extracts from an old minute book: The Edinburgh Sugar house Company 1763-1773*, p. 14

89. George Chandler, *Liverpool* (Batsford: 1957) p. 332

90. Liverpool Maritime Museum, D/Earle/4/1-2, Reel 12

91. Liverpool Maritime Museum, D/Earle/4/4, 20 August 1785 Jonathan Blundell died and the ironmonger, William Earle, became the senior partner

92. Today Campbell Street and Duke Street mark the site

93. LRO DDX 158/2

94. W. Enfield, *An Essay towards the History of Liverpool, 1773* Facsimile (Rondo publications: 1972) p. 88

95. This was the area where John Wright's refinery, later to become Tate and Sons, was established in 1859

96. Red Cross Street, the site of the Danvers refinery, was built across Tarleton's field in the 1660s

97. Doreen Heckedy, *Bound for a New World*, (TLCHS 1995, vol. 144) p. 121

98. Frank Tyrer ed. *The Great Diurnal of Nicholas Blundell, vol. 1 1702-1711* (The Record Society 1968) p. 66

99. Another advertisement for rum appeared in the Liverpool Courier of 1768, and this included a few hogsheads of French clay'd sugar – refined in clay moulds.

100. A. C. Cumming *Extracts from an old minute book. The Edinburgh Sugar House Company 1763-1773*, p. 5

101. The sum that was charged for the lease, makes an interesting comparison with the accounts of George Campbell & Co. mentioned earlier, and also with the various bequests of the other refiners and puts those bequeasts into perspective

102. Thomas Beckwith was involved in the Gildart refinery with William Beckwith – possibly his son. *Lewis's Directory 1790*

103. This report was made between 1763 and his death in 1769

104. George Chandler, *Liverpool* (Batsford: 1957) p. 332

105. Anthony Hugill, Sugar and *All that ... The History of Tate and Lyle*, (London: Gentry Books, 1978) p. 30

106. S. Haggerty 'Liverpool trading community' in M. J. Power 'The Growth of Liverpool" in *Essays in Liverpool History*, (Liverpool: 1992) pp. 21-37 in TLCHS Vol. 151, 2002, p. 100

Chapter 3: The Chester Refineries

107. First mentioned in Chalmer's biographical dictionary in 1816. Kerry Downes, *Sir John Vanburgh, a Biography* (London: Sidgwick and Jackson 1987) p. 31

108. This friendship continued at least until Giles death in 1683 when Anthony was one of the witnesses to his will

109. Kerry Downes, *Sir John Vanbrugh;a Biography*, p. 35

110. See the account in the chapter on Ormskirk's refinery

111. Leave lookers were both inspectors of weights and measures and the collectors of dues for the city. Chester City R.O. A/B/2/189

112. *Ibid.* A/B/2/195v

113. *Ibid.* A/B/197

114. *Ibid.* A/B/3/3

115. *Ibid.* A/B/3/5v

116. Kerry Downes *Sir John Vanbrugh;a Biography*, p. 35, 38

117. CRO EDC 5 (1682) No. 6, Chester (St Bridget's)

118. Rolls of the Freemen of the City of Chester (LCRS: 1906) No.51

119. CRO WCW Samuel Henthorne 1695

120. See the chapter on the Liverpool sugar refiners

121. He was cited on a marriage bond in 1718 CRO

122. CRO H/76 Hincks Papers, 1687. Will of Edward Hincks

123. This lane (later street) lies to the west of Bridge Street close to the River Dee

124. CRO H/8 H/9 Hincks Papers 1752

125. CRO H/10 Hincks papers 1753

126. CRO H/22 Hincks Papers 1757

127. CRO H/20, H/21 Hincks Papers 1757

128. In 1778 Joseph Parr of Warrington entered into an agreement with Robert Hesketh another merchant from Chester, to found a sugar refining company in Warrington. See Chapter on Warrington refineries

129. CRO Hincks Papers, H/56, 1758

130. Liverpool R.O. E190/1337/7

131. R. Pares, 'The London Sugar Market', Econ. Hist. Review IX No. 2 1956, quoted in Wilson Charles, *England's Apprenticeship 1623-1763* (Longmans, Green & Co.: 1965) p. 275

132. It must have been customary that, if the distillers could pay cash, they could purchase their molasses at a cheaper rate – '24s money instead of 25s or 26s' in some kind of bill of exchange

133. CRO Hincks Papers H/59 1758

134. *Ibid.*

135. CRO Hincks Papers H/59 1758

136. CRO Hincks Papers H/62 15 April 1758

137. CRO Hincks Papers H/61 1758

138. CRO Hincks Papers H/ 108 1764

139. CRO Hincks Papers H/ 29 Dec. 1764

140. CRO Hincks Papers H/103 The solicitors' itemised bill for their services

141. CRO Hincks Papers H/86 1770

142. CRO Hincks Papers H/28 1772

143. CRO Hincks papers H/72 1775-6

144. CRO Hincks Papers H/73, H/74, 1777

145. CRO Hincks Papers H/80 1777

146. CRO Hincks Papers H/75 1777

147. CRO Hincks Papers H/90 1778

148. CRO Hincks family papers. D5879

149. CRO Hincks Papers H/67

150. This course was also taken by the Crosfield family who moved from grocery in Warrington to sugar refining in Lancaster

151. Ashley Baynton-Williams, *Town and City Maps of the British Isles 1800-1855*, map of Chester *c.* 1800 by Cole and Roper p. 22

Chapter 4: Refineries in the South of the Region

152. Christopher Morris, ed. *The Journeys of Celia Fiennes* (Cresset Press: 1947), p. 184

153. For instance LRO QSP 367/19, QSP375/6, QSP 416/13, QSP 722/27

154. LRO WCW James Berry 1686. Evidently the appraisers had found several casks with a small amount of unrefined sugar remaining in them and estimated there would be two pounds in them

155. This inn has now been converted into cottages and stands between the roundabout on the Ormskirk- Skelmersdale- Rainford road and the M58 motorway in Bickerstaffe. See also the testimony of George Hulme in PRO PL27/1

156. This quotation and those following are taken from the documentation of the trial at Lancaster Assizes –Woosey v Barton Laithwaite. PRO PL6/34/37

157. See the testimony of Ambrose Sharples of Chester, one of the witnesses in trial at the Assizes. PRO PL6/34/37 North Meols and Preston

158. E. Bland *Annals of Southport and District* (Guardian: 1903) p. 27

159. LRO DRL 1/57

160. James Barron, *A History of the Ribble Navigation* (Corporation of Preston: 1938) p. 48

161. Francis A. Bailey, *A History of Southport* (Angus Downie: 1955) p. 40

162. That was the conclusion drawn by Peter Aughton who claimed that Liverpool slave ships landed there Peter Aughton, *North Meols and Southport A History*, (Carnegie: 1988) p. 77. It was not unusual for warehouses for sugar to be set up in places that seem remote from the trade today. For instance in 1741 a warehouse was built at Skippool on the banks of the river Wyre for goods from Barbados, but there is no mention of a sugar house in that location.

163. LRO WCW Richard Parke of Formby 1674

164. When he left Nicholas tipped two of the sailors presumably in acknowledgement of some unnamed service.

165. PRO E190/1382/2 RO4/9 1711/12- 1714/1715

166. LRO WCW John Hesketh 1767

167. *R. R. Angerstein's Illustrated Travel Diary 1753-1755* Industry in England and Wales from Swedish perspective illustrated by Torsten and Peter Berg, (Science Museum: 2001) p. 295. Warrington

168. Letter to Richard Norris 8 Jan 1697 Norris Papers [CS (OS) 1846] pp. 37-9

169. *The Archaeology of Warrington's Past* by Shelagh Grealey, (Warrington Development Corporation: 1976) p. 20

170. Warrington Library *The Pattens of Warrington and the Copper Industry*. Talk given by J. R. Harris to the Warrington Archaeologial and Historical Society, p. 7

171. CRO D/Hincks 56

172. Bank Hall was bought by the council in 1872 for £22,000 and converted into WarringtonTown Hall "Warrington and the Mid-Mersey Valley, E. J. Morten (Morton: 1971) p. 139

173. Chamberlayne *The Present State of Great Britain* (1755) quoted in Crowe, Austin M. *Warrington Ancient and Modern* (Beamont Press: 1947) p. 115

174. According to an article in the Warrington Guardian Nov. 6th 1936.

175. Letter from Manesty to Wilson of the Chester Sugar House `I would not be hasty as if these orders are complyd with by Mr Marsden & Lancaster Sugar house, the Country will be base & yours be called for at Higher rates'. CRO Hincks Papers H/56

176. Warrington Guardian 6 November 1936

177. Joseph Parr had previously had financial dealings with Robert Hesketh, when he borrowed £500 at 5 per cent p.a in 1761, but exactly what else was involved in that transaction is unclear.

178. Deed of covenant for levying a fine by Mr and Mrs Kerfoot. Warrington Library MS 1162 Box LW15

179. Warrington Central Library The Lyons Deeds MSS 1162 Box LW1

180. PRO C113/75

181. Crowe, Austin M. *Warrington Ancient and Modern* (Beamont Press: 1947) p. 146

182. For details of the construction of this navigation see Charles Hadfield & Gordon Biddle, *The Canals of North West England vol. 1*,(Newton Abbot, David & Charles, 1970) p. 17

183. V. I. Tomlinson 'Early Warehouses on Manchester Waterways' TLCAS 71 1961 p. 143

184. The site is occupied now by the Granada Centre and the site of the sugar house itself is the car park serving the Centre

185. V. I. Tomlinson, 'Salford Activities connected with the Bridgewater Canal' TLCAAS, vol. LXVI 1956, p. 59

186. *Ibid.* p. 77

187. Slater's Directory for Manchester 1869

188. J. Radcliffe, *Directory of Manchester and District 1781*

Chapter 5: Sugar Refining in Lancaster and Whitehaven

189. J. D. Marshall ed et al. *The Autobiography of William Stout of Lancaster 1665-1752*, p. 144-45

190. The Corporation Act banned people who did not take Communion in the Church of England from taking office. Also the Quakers were barred by their refusal to take the required oath. Nicholas Morgan, 'The Social and Political Relations of the Lancaster Quaker Community 1688-1740' in Michael Mullett ed., *Early Lancaster Friends* CNWRS, No. 5, 1978, p. 23

191. J. L. Nickall ed., *The Journal of George Fox* (CUP: 1952) p. 120

192. Kenneth H. Docton, 'Lancaster' TLCHS vol. 109 1957 p. 74

193. Stallage was the annual payment for the privilege of keeping a stall in the weekly market. See Illustration of stallage rolls in Andrew White, ed. *History of Lancaster* (Keele University Press: 1993) p. 81

194. This token resembles a medieval coin with the symbol of the 'Lamb and Flag' or Angus Dei. Michael Mullett, 'Reformation and Renewal 1450-1690' in White ed. *A History of Lancaster* p. 80

195. Marshall, ed. *The Autobiography of William Stout*, p. 145

196. *Ibid.* p. 145

197. For more information about the development of Sunderland Point visit Lancaster Maritime Museum; also see R. C. Jarvis, 'Some Records of the Port of Lancaster', TLCAS. Vol.58 1945-46, pp. 117-158; M. M. Schofield, *Outlines of an Economic History of Lancaster from 1680-1860*, Lancaster branch of the Historical Association, 2 vols. 1946, 1951

198. Joan Wilkinson, *The Letters of Thomas Langton, flax merchant of Kirkham 1771-1788*,CS 1994 vol. 38, p. 26

199. Nigel Dalziel, 'Trade and Transition 1690-1815' in Andrew White, ed. *The History of Lancaster*, pp. 93-94

200. M. M. Schofield, 'The Letter Book of Benjamin Satterthwaite of Lancaster 1737-1744', THSLC. Vol. 113 1961, p. 132

201. LRO WCW. Will of Abraham Rawlinson of Lancaster 1780.

202. LRO DDGa/18 Militia Lists for Lancaster

203. CRO H/61 Hincks Papers for 1758

204. LRO FRL 2/1/11 Society of Friends Removal Certificates for Lancaster for 1742, 1762

205. See the chapter on the Chester refineries.

206. LRO WCW Will of Myles Birket of Lancaster 1785

207. See portrait in Dalziel, Trade and Transition ... in White ed., *A History of Lancaster* p. 96

208. In 1752 Astley was registered as part-owner of the Clifton of Preston. He lost a part cargo of sugar when the Martha of Lancaster was wrecked. Schofield, *Letterbook* p. 136

209. Marriage Bonds of Lancaster 1746-1755 (RSLC Vol. 115) p. 48

210. Margaret Fell of Swarthmoor Hall married George Fox in October 1669

211. He died aged 38 in 1824 and his gravestone can be seen in the Priory churchyard

212. The Lancaster Freemen and Apprentice Books 15 July 1760. Schofield *Letterbook*, p. 136

213. These deeds are held in Manchester Central Library Local Studies Dept. No 245a 7b 1766, and No. 246 176

214. For further details of the sale see the chapter on the refineries in Warrington

215. W. C. Braithwaite, *The Second Period of Quakerism* (CUP: 1961) p. 596

216. LRO WCW Will of Abraham Rawlinson 1780

217. *Free Burgesses of Lancaster* RSLC Vol. 90, 1938, LRO; WCW Will of John Addison of Lancaster 1788

218. Nigel Dalziel, 'Trade and Transition 1690-1815' in Andrew White ed., *A History of Lancaster* p. 128

219. The Manchester Directory for 1794 recorded Robert Grierson as a fustian manufacturer in Bayley's Court

220. LRO WCW Will of James Hargreaves of Lancaster 1804

221. A. E. Musson, *Enterprise in Soap and Chemicals, Crosfields of Warrington* (MUP: 1963) p. 8-9

222. Nigel Dalziel, *Trade and Transition 1690-1815*, pp. 133-34

223. A. E. Musson, *Enterprise in Soap and Chemicals*, (MUP: 1965) pp. 5-9 Whitehaven

224. *Whitehaven, a new structure for a restoration town*, Municipal Borough of Whitehaven Report 1980, p. 16

225. PRO E 134/3 Jas II Mich. No. 33 quoted in Christine Church *Sir John Lowther and Whitehaven* thesis 1991

226. For a fuller account of the coastal trade see A. Eaglesham,*The growth and influence of the West Cumberland Shipping Industry 1660-1800* PhD thesis, University of Lancaster, p. 108

227. D. R. Hainsmith ed., *The correspondence of Sir John Lowther of Whitehaven 1693-1698* (OUP: 1982) Letter 505 p. 567

228. *Whitehaven 1660-1800* The Royal Commission on the Historical Monuments of England 1991 HMSO p. 18

229. Cumbrian Record Office, Carlisle, D/Lons/W2/1/45, Letter no. 52

230. Cumbrian Record Office, Carlisle, D/Lons/W2?45 Letter no. 55

231. Cumbria Record Office, Carlisle D/Lons/W2/1, Letter no. 57. Barwis, Berwis and Barwise were fairly common surnames in Cumbria at this time

232. G. P. Jones, *Two Hudleston and Senhouse Account Books*, Humphrey Senhouse 1669-1738 Day Book 1699-1704T.C.,W.A.A.S N.S., LXVI p. 330

233. Eaglesham,*The Growth and Influence of the West Cumberland Shipping ...* p. 92

234. Cumbrian Record Office Carlisle, D/Lons/W2/1/89 letter No. 12

235. Cumbrian Record Office, Carlisle D/Lons/W2/72, Letter No. 11

236. J. V. Beckett *Coal and Tobacco 1660-1770* (CUP 1981), p. 174-5

237. *Ibid.* p. 146

238. *North Country Life in 18th Century Vol. II*, Cumberland and Westmorland 1700-1830 (OUP 1965) p. 45

239. Cumbrian Record Office, Carlisle, D/Lons/W2/1/84, Letter 54

240. Melinda Elder, *The Slave Trade* (Rybrun: 1992) p. 102. A tierce contained approximately 35 gallons

241. *R. R. Angerstein's Illustrated Travel Diary 1753-1755* (Science Museum: 2002) p. 281

242. *Journal of the House of Commons*, 26. Geo. II March 10th p. 709

243. A. N. Rigg, *Cumbrian Slavery and the Textile Industrial Revolution* p. 164

244. *North Country Life in the 18th Century Vol. II*, Cumberland and Westmorland 1700-1830 (OUP 1965), p. 349

245. Commercial Directory 1821-22 p. 329, Parson and White's Directory of Cumberland and Westmorland for 1829 Quoted in Rigg p. 165

246. I am indebted to the staff at 'The Rum Story' for information on the Jefferson family and the distillery. Unfortunately a fire in 1814 destroyed the early documents which might have referred to the link with early sugar refining in Whitehaven

Acknowledgements

I owe a deep debt of gratitude to so many friends and fellow historians who have helped me to produce this final version of my research. The staff at the various record offices ranging from Carlisle to Chester and the curators of the museum in Chester have been so patient, offering suggestions and showing an interest in my work as I delved among their records. Then friends and even acquaintances have encouraged me constantly with "How's the Sugar book going along?" and in drawing my attention to any remote mention of sugar refining. Many of these hints revealed gems of information which I was able to incorporate into my work. The person to whom I owe my love of research must be thanked individually. He is Professor Michael Mullett of LancasterUniversity, who supported me along the way and suggested the title for this book. Then I must thank the council of the Athenaeum in Liverpool, who have allowed me to publish illustrations from their collection. However, perhaps the greatest debt is owed to the Historic Society of Lancashire and Cheshire who awarded me a grant to enable me to publish my work. The greatest and a final vote of thanks must go to my late husband who tirelessly accompanied me through all these years of research. Thank you all.

Index